Accounting's Changing Role in Social Conflict

Cheryl R. Lehman

ACCOUNTING'S CHANGING ROLE IN SOCIAL CONFLICT

Cheryl R. Lehman

Markus Wiener Publishing, Inc.
New York & Princeton

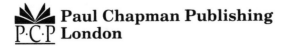

Paul Chapman Publishing
London

For information write to:

Markus Wiener Publishing, Inc.
225 West 34th Street, New York, NY 10001

For the United Kingdom and Continental Europe write to:

Paul Chapman Publishing, Ltd.
144 Liverpool Road, London N1 1LA
Tel. 071-609-5315

LIBRARY OF CONGRESS CATALOGING-IN-PUBLICATION DATA

Lehman, Cheryl R.
  Accounting's Changing Role in Social Conflict / by Cheryl R. Lehman
  Includes bibliographical references.
  ISBN 1-55876-030-X
  1. Accounting—Social aspects.   2. Social conflict.   I. Title.
  HF5657.L394   1992   91-47864 CIP
  657—dc20

BRITISH LIBRARY CATALOGUING IN PUBLICATION DATA

Lehman, Cheryl R.
  Accounting's Changing Role in Social Conflict
  I. Title
  657

  ISBN 1853961698

Printed in the United States of America

In loving memory of my father, the printer,
Harold J. Shoulson

CONTENTS

PREFACE
AND ACKNOWLEDGMENTS

During the years of writing this book, there have been considerable changes in the academic milieu of accounting, the professional environment, and my own theoretical development. "The Beginning," for me, was my dissertation research at New York University, where I was fortunate enough to encounter a variety of intellectual protagonists. They were among the early challengers of the received methodologies of accounting and the social sciences. These scholars provided insight and stimulation by which I could reassess the social role of a subject, hitherto treated as a technique, and explore accounting as a socially constituted and contested terrain. Colleagues familiar with this epistemic genre will recognize these scholars—Tony Tinker, Marilyn Neimark, Barbara Merino, Jim Ratliff, Paul Shrivastava, Richard Brief, George Sorter, and Joshua Ronen—and acknowledge the discipline's debt to them.

This book is an act of revenge for the hours spent learning conventional accounting. This revenge is in the form of a critique of the traditional canon. The social roles of accounting, although articulated by a growing arena of academics, is treated as non-problematic by most members of the traditional accounting community. This book not only challenges the presumptions of conventional rhetoric on its own grounds, it also contributes to the radical accounting research project. Viewing accounting as a discourse, a form of social signification, and a mode of adjudicating in wealth conflicts—privileging and enhancing certain interests, denying and repressing others—are among the themes examined here.

The research for this book benefited from the good counsel and advice of many colleagues, friends, and family. Marilyn Neimark's talent, resource, and knowledge of the social roles of accounting was a significant source of ideas from the early stages of this work. I am indebted to her for her endless enthusiasm, friendship, and stimulation while I pursued this project. Penny Ciancanelli, Theresa Hammond, and Leslie Oakes each uniquely inspired, provoked, nurtured, and supported me in countless ways. I could not ask for more intellectually and spiritually thoughtful colleagues and friends. Barbara Merino's contribution to challenging the history of accounting, and her commitment to doctoral research, has been illuminating. Cheryl Payer taught me the joy of having one's own personal view, continually reassessing received ideas along any spectrum—left or right.

Patricia Arnold, Abe Briloff, David Cooper, Sonja Gallhofer, James Guthrie, Leslie Gruss, James Haslam, Nick Kozlov, Anne Loft, Tony Lowe, Carol McKeen, Susan McAnn, Rob Nehmer, Wanda Orlankowski, Lee Parker, Ann Pushkin, Michael Rosen, Sheldon Tesser, Paula Thomas, Paul Williams, Mark Young, Sara Zug, and the MFIV reading group have all contributed toward mentoring, stimulating, and supporting me. The enduring and close friendships of Ellen Lus and Caryn Streicher Dombek have been particularly important to my wellbeing. My family— mother, sister, and brother—are to be thanked for letting me "get on with it."

Ralph Polimeni (Chairperson of the Department of Accounting and Business Law), Herman Berliner (Provost and Dean of Faculties), and many other individuals at Hofstra University supported this project. Russell Moore, Fahrettin Okcabol, and Linda Zwiren have been ideal colleagues and close friends. Sylvia Federici, Estelle Gellman, Selma Greenberg, and Linda Longmire have been extraordinary role models. Pauline Parish and Cathy Newfield contributed to data collection and administrative matters. Special thanks go to Sylvia Zaino, whose energy and warmth is greatly appreciated.

Behind every book on political agitation there stands a politically agitated publisher. Markus Wiener reigns supreme in the volume of critical accounting works that he has brought to the market. My gratitude also extends to Danny Markus, copy editor, for his perceptive and thoughtful improvements.

My most cherished acknowledgment goes to Tony Tinker, my closest and dearest friend, colleague, and soul mate. His enduring intellectual creativity, his commitment to the subject matter of this book, and his emotional support and encouragement have been invaluable. No other person understands as clearly what this book means to me, both academically and personally.

This book is dedicated to my father, Harold J. Shoulson. His loss was an untimely passing for a man whose energy, wit, and passion for his family continued to flourish. As a printer by trade, he would be proud and delighted to see this work published. His confidence in me, his caring and love, and his pleasure in my successes—large and small—strengthened me throughout our relationship. It is with much joy that I dedicate this book to him.

CHAPTER I

INTRODUCTION

Accounting practice has always been afflicted by financial collapses and controversies, yet accounting literature traditionally eschews the social conflicts underlying these upheavals. Examples of such disputes abound: third world debts of more than $1 trillion, savings and loans bailouts of up to $1.4 trillion, and finance wizards' fines for hundreds of millions of dollars. Such calamities prompt the courts and the media to point accusingly in the direction of a number of suspects—the banking community, regulatory agents, career diplomats, shrewd politicians, and misguided economists. How is it that the accounting profession has largely escaped notice? In all of these transgressions, the role of the accountant—as arbitrator, as public policy maker, as legitimator, or as myth maker—deserves scrutiny and investigation. It is appropriate to ask, "Where were the accountants?"

By theorizing about accounting practice in a social and political vacuum, controversies involving stockholders, managers, pension holders, employees, consumers, the state, and others have been misapprehended, silenced, or given anomalous meaning. To balance the debate and to devise policies that are worthy of the profession's public mandate, we must move beyond posturing about "objectivity" and "efficiency" and examine the social genesis of accounting. This book begins that investigation by considering accounting's participation in contemporary financial events and offering a framework for systematically exploring accounting's role in social conflict.

Accounting's influence spans the full range of our life experience, from the mundane to the globally consequential. Consider the array of accounting data: estimating the productivity of robots, pricing shares in management buyouts, forecasting costs of strategic defense systems, comparing pollution control costs and benefits, weighing health care options and strategies, and planning playgrounds for inner city schools. Do accountants embrace the social implications manifest in the data? Most often she or he is unfamiliar with critical thinking and lacking in political and social acumen, having been subject to rote learning of FASB (Financial Accounting Standards Board) standards and a detached educational experience. Most disquieting of all is that the accountant as a caring and knowledgeable socially oriented citizen is virtually an unknown species.

Accounting's privileged access to specialized information regarding corporate and financial activity places it in a unique position of power and knowledge. When accounting is viewed merely as a static set of rules, standards, or data crunching, innumerable opportunities are overlooked for using procedures to recast and rationalize key decisions.

Whether accounting is incidental or crucial in these social choices is a debate that rallies a wide spectrum of beliefs. Market study theorists contend accounting "doesn't matter," reasoning that capital markets readily impound available information into stock prices. Accounting's irrelevance stems from its historical nature—the information is already available from other sources, thus stock prices already reflect the information. Nor is the market fooled by superficial accounting reporting changes; such information is inconsequential to the reasonably sophisticated investor.

The irrelevance of accounting emerges for others from its condition as "a technology of foolishness: a ritualistic kind of playfulness and experimentalization" (Cooper, 1983). On this side of the spectrum, theorists ridicule the potential of accounting as social action, contending that if we were to change the world, we certainly would not start with accounting (Gray, et al., 1987). This begs the question that accounting is not related to nothingness, but what its presence promotes, enhances, denies, or destroys. The existence and dissemination of accounting, as the language of business, as a sign system, as a social practice, and as ideology, elevates accounting beyond the trite and trivial, and recognizes its role as a ritualized method of resolving conflict.

Aligned with a different stance are those claiming a true measure of account or accountability for a given decision indeed exists. Accounting's task is to report on this true underlying economic value as a form of representational faithfulness. This view denies accounting measures as biased or aligned with certain constituencies, claiming that by reporting facts, accounting is socially neutral, objective, and dispassionate.

Our claim is a more dynamic, interactive, socially constituted view of the subject, one that we call dialectic. Accounting both reflects and affects the struggles in the social, corporate, financial, domestic, and global spheres; it is neither an insignificant player nor a mere bearer of the facts.

These many facets of accounting are the subject of this book, and in this introduction we present scenarios of discord within the global and domestic community over which vast resources, commercial activity, and social policies have been transferred and transformed. Although the narrative of an accounting role is rarely articulated in the popular press when these stories are told, the task of this introduction is to begin to illuminate accounting's influence and intervention in these affairs, and restore a pride of place of accounting's social role.

Global Debt to Pay

The urgency of the global debt and banking crises is exemplified by discord in the U.S. Congress and ruptures in domestic and international arenas. Claims against the FDIC regarding bank failures and bailouts have reached record proportions. Estimates are that $600 billion to $1.4 trillion will be required to bail out the thrifts, equivalent to more than three times the U.S. government (federal) deficit. Commercial banks, overburdened with hundreds of billions of dollars of inactive and unsecured loans, prompted Chemical Bank president Thomas S. Johnson to warn in 1986 of "the possibility of a nightmarish domino effect as every creditor ransacks the globe attempting to locate his collateral." Developing countries face negative or minimal growth, prohibitive rates of inflation, mounting fiscal deficits, and devastating cuts in social programs.

How are we to explain the fragility of global financial markets, in which Third World debts are estimated at $1 trillion? Have disclosure policies revealed crucial interdependencies, the deteriorating credit-worthiness of debtors and imminent insolvencies? In contrast to 1973 figures, when developing countries received nearly twice as much money from official creditors (e.g., the World Bank), a majority of global loans are now owed to private commercial banks. Default by any one or a combination of the large Latin American countries could lead to the bankruptcy of more than one of the large U.S. money center banks.

Bank Accounting Practices

The 1933–1934 Securities Acts, requiring large corporations to employ certified public accountants to audit their financial statements, conferred on the profession a congressionally backed monopolistic control over its market. With some minor exceptions, banks were included within the financial reporting and auditing provision of the acts. For a bank to recognize a loan to a customer under Generally Accepted Accounting Principles (GAAP) as an asset, and subsequently to recognize as profit the interest earned on the loan, repayment must be reasonably assured, and all work must have been substantially accomplished. An auditor is obligated under GAAP to see that these conditions are met before giving a clean (unqualified) opinion on the accounts. If conditions are not met, a provision against the likely loss should be made and, as soon as the receivable is deemed uncollectible, it should be written off against the provision.

Although accounting procedures exist for exposing uncollectible loans and potential defaults, banks have avoided disclosing losses since the early 1980s. U.S. banks are reluctant to write-off debt because bank reserves are insufficient to absorb such a write-down and meet the minimum capital requirements specified by federal authorities. In many cases just before some loans are about to go into a non-performing status (loans with overdue interest of over 90 days), additional loans are made to debtors, merely to enable them to pay the interest owed to the creditor. Non-performing status (part of a multi-stage process for recognizing potential defaults) requires banks to subtract as much as six months' interest income and to establish loan loss reserves for problem loans. By avoiding non-performing status, banks continue recognizing interest income on troubled loans. Little attention is given to the deteriorating economic condition of the debtor, which is the final determinant of the value of the loan.

FASB #15, "Accounting by Debtors and Creditors for Troubled Debt Restructuring" (1977), describes one of the generally accepted accounting practices applicable to banks. The statement does *not* prescribe write-downs on renegotiated debt as long as the undiscounted future cash flows are the same before and after the debt restructuring. Thus if all future interest is waived on a $100 million loan, and repayment of the principal is deferred to decades into the future, no loss is acknowledged under FASB #15.

The FASB's decision is controversial. Two distinguished members of the Board wrote a strong minority opinion stressing the distortions such an omission creates. They claim that by ignoring recognition of a substantive consequence—the event of relinquishing rights in a debt restructuring—the FASB is taking a backward step. Numerous releases in the press asserted that the Board succumbed to pressure from special interests, most notably the defense and banking sectors. As the statement was debated during New York City's financial crisis in the 1970s, large money center banks lobbied hard against the original exposure draft, which would have required significant write-downs in loans to the City.

The profession's track record in banking is currently under scrutiny for approving as financially healthy banks declared insolvent only months after the clean audit report. Government auditors have accused five accounting firms, including three of the Big Six of failing to uncover and disclose bad financial practices at six thrifts that eventually failed, by allegedly overlooking problems such as bad loans and regulatory violations. Leaders of the U.S. Congress House Banking Committee accuse the accounting firms as being "derelict in their responsibility to sound early alarms about impending disasters" (*Newsday*, February 3, 1989). Although accountants have been under fire before, "never before have accountants faced anything as brutal, or as potentially costly, as this onslaught . . . many are wondering whether these hard nosed pencil-pushing professionals lost what they valued the most: their cool logic, their skeptical air, their independent voice" (*The New York Times,* March 12, 1989).

Additional bankruptcies and defaults have been avoided up to now because of the prompt and energetic rescue by the U.S. government, central bankers, the International Monetary Fund (IMF) and the World Bank, but clearly these lenders of last resort cannot extend rescue operations indefinitely. Throughout the 1960s and 1970s the control of central banks over the monetary system declined, as did the IMF's influence over world liquidity—although the IMF retained its prominence as lender of last resort. The complex regulatory mechanism of balancing private and public information regarding international markets increasingly relied on private verification of these transactions through, for example, audited financial statements. Between 1982 and 1987, after the unprecedented 1982 default by Mexico, banks continued to lend to troubled debtors, increasing outstanding loans from $568 billion to $1 trillion, the equivalent of half the annual national income and one and a half times the annual exports of the poorest countries in the world.

A debtor's ability to repay a loan lies in what the debtor uses the loan for. Productive investment in agriculture or industry is likely to yield a return that assures repayment of interest and principal. In addition to the cash flows these investments might generate, they also create real assets that could be liquidated to repay the loan in the event of default. It has been estimated that one third of Third World debt has been subject to capital flight— funds earmarked for investment in a country that end up in private bank accounts abroad. Examples of loans used for private consumption include those to Jean-Claude Duvalier, to Manuel Noriega, and the Marcoses. It is the duty of a bank lending officer and the auditor to inquire into circumstances in order to ascertain the "real" value of the loan and the credit-worthiness of the debtor.

GAAP has a markdown-to-market rule (the Lower of Cost or Market [LCM] rule) for inventory, investments in shares, and other assets. The precautionary spirit of this rule is obvious: it is intended that balance sheet values should be conservatively stated, and thus income and earnings (and thus dividends) should be restricted by these conservative values.

In the case of Third World loan assets, exchange values established in the secondary market provide an indication of the market value of such assets. Banks have consistently ignored these market values and have thus violated the spirit of the LCM rule. In some cases the differences are dramatic: the secondary market quoted (in November 1987) five cents per dollar for Peruvian debt, thirty-five cents for Argentina, thirty-three cents for Ecuador, fifty cents for Mexico, and thirty-nine cents for Brazil.

Costs of the International Debt Crises

There is a close relationship between the international debt and trade deficit problems plaguing the U.S. economy. Debtor nations, in order to service their debts and obtain hard currency (U.S. dollars), have slashed imports, including U.S. goods, and boosted exports by reducing prices—competing with the United States. This is good news for servicing the debt, but not for American industry, the agricultural sector, or U.S. labor. A study conducted by the New York Federal Reserve Bank in 1983 forecasted that nearly 400,000 jobs would be lost "as a result of declining merchandise exports to Latin America." Wharton Economics puts the loss at an estimated 800,000 jobs. One economist claims, "The unemployment and industrial disruption in the U.S. rust belt are not due solely to industrial deficiencies. . . . U.S. workers may lose jobs so that Brazilian debts to Swiss bankers that manage accounts for Arab interests can be" repaid. Bailing out the savings and loan industry is expected to cost each U.S. taxpayer thousands of dollars over the next decade.

The burden of the debt in debtor countries falls on the poor and the working class as it does in the United States (Payer, 1991). In countries with standards of living well below that of the United States, and those whose standards declined during the 1980s, the call for belt tightening by the IMF and the World Bank has fallen on deaf ears. Citing the poverty and misery of the Peruvian people, former president Alan Garcia, addressing the United Nations in September 1985 claimed, "We are faced with a dramatic choice: it is either debt or democracy." Brazil's then-president, José Sarney, addressed the audience claiming that "under the weight of an enormous foreign debt, the countries of the region [are witness to] recession, unemployment, inflation, increased poverty, and violence" (*The New York Times,* September 24, 1985).

What is the scope of responsibility of accountants and auditors in situations such as that described above? We do not wish to prejudge the answer to this question here, but we do feel it is an appropriate question to pose.

Application of accounting principles and procedures for income recognition, asset valuation, and conservatism should coincide with reasonable assurance of loan collections, and income earned should reflect expected cash flows. In assessing the timing for recognizing events in the accounts of banks, auditors must ask at what stage in negotiations does a bank have a new loan asset. When should the interest portion be recognized as a profit? What evidence is sufficient for writing down loans and recognizing losses? Has appropriate judgement been applied in regard to Third World loans?

An auditor's attestation inevitably privileges some and deprives others, and in the global financial markets, the profession sanctions the transfer of wealth between numerous constituencies. Bank managers, First and Third World elites, and others may have been more culpable than accountants. Yet in our task, to examine accounting's role, it is reasonable to ask: Have ineffectual accounting standards and procedures exacerbated the crises and increased eventual losses?

Boom and Bust of Mergers

Many of the woes plaguing the finance and banking sector emerge not from international practices, but from the domestic merger mania of the 1980s and the fallout effect of the main source of merger financing—junk bonds. Many of these junk bonds, crucial in funding the escalating consolidation of firms, have proved to be worthless, driving giants of the trading industry, such as Drexel Burnham Lambert, Inc. into bankruptcy, and causing a rippling effect of huge financial losses and unemployment within the securities industry. Ivan Boesky and Michael Milken, once the most renowned traders in securities and junk bonds, have become infamous because of the government's indictments, fines, and jail time.

In the case of First Executive Life, a California insurer seized by regulators in April 1991, hundreds of investors stand to lose a sizable portion of the $1.85 billion invested into what they thought were conservative municipal bonds (*Fortune,* May 20, 1991). First Executive's junk assets are known to be far less than the values at which they are being carried—and at which they must be carried in order to meet claims. Just as First Executive's shareholders have seen the value of their shares plunge as the marketplace has rendered its verdict on its junk assets, so too are policy holders at risk. With $59 billion of insurance in force covering 200,000 policy holders, and assets inadequate to cover these claims, there is every likelihood that huge losses are inevitable (*Barron's,* April 1, 1991). It has been claimed that some of these consequences are the result of an intricate system of mystification of "real" values, and the accounting numbers and procedures used to justify "the art of the deal" (as discussed by Donald Trump).

Who wins in transactions involving junk bonds, takeovers, and management buyouts? Texaco, Walt Disney Productions, St. Regis Corporation, and Warner Communications, to name a few, avoided takeovers by entitling five main bidders to share a total of $486 million of profits and have incurred hundreds of millions of dollars in legal costs in the process (*Business Week,* March 4, 1985). "But most spectacularly," states Barron's, regarding management's prospering at the expense of the shareholders, "there's Time, Inc., now Time Warner, whose directors refused to let shareholders vote on an offer that would have paid them a big premium, a premium that looks even more lucrative given the stock's fall of almost 100 points" (*Barron's,* December 24, 1990). The profit earned by T. Boone Pickens in his "unsuccessful" bid for Gulf Oil Company in 1984 has been estimated at $760 million, and his bid for Phillips Petroleum Company (1985), brought him $115 million of profit. In addition, Phillips is obligated to pay out to legal and financial advisers of Pickens a total of $50 million for their services (*Financial Times,* March 15, 1985; *The New York Times,* March 5, 1985).

Praise and support for takeover campaigns emerged from a diverse list of financial advisers, analysts, well-known economists, and finance and law professors, claiming these settlements and transfers ensure efficiency of management, forcing them to be responsive to shareholders. The success of Pickens' shareholders, in holding out for a better offer from management, has been hailed as a victory for shareholders, with Icahn describing the settlement as "an important milestone for shareholder democracy" (*Financial Times,* March 15, 1985). Since takeovers originate, claim the raiders, because management has underutilized a company's resources, takeover bids are a new form of natural market regulation, constraining management to productively utilize assets entrusted to them by shareholders.

Not everyone celebrates this turn of events. Harold Williams, former Chairman of the Securities and Exchange Commission, claims that the takeover activities are a "major disaster for shareholder democracy" (*Financial Times,* March 15, 1985). These bids are hardly seen as free market regulation; rather they are costly and destabilizing to financial markets and the economy. The loss to shareholders is clearly demonstrated when the takeover bid proves to be "greenmail," a form of corporate blackmail; the greenmailer's shares are purchased back from the company at a price not available to shareholders. The final outcome—the perpetuation of management, inefficient or otherwise, and frequently a weakened financial position for the company—is a dubious victory for the shareholders. Takeover bids, even when they are not in the form of greenmail, are still a cause for concern: companies avoid takeovers by assuming towering debt burdens while management inefficiencies increase as they pursue short-run strategies to avoid takeovers, and ignore long-term objectives.

The costs incurred for mergers are staggering—bidding wars frequently force successful buyers to pay excessive premiums and incur enormous debt. These debts often cause an immediate liquidity crisis, and are only payable by selling off the most lucrative assets of the acquired firm. As more and more debt is incurred, the economy, unable to extend the necessary credit, is fueled toward escalating rates of interest for all forms of borrowing, particularly in cases of greater risk. Long-term innovation and productivity are jeopardized. As firms pursue short-run profits, they become caught in pursuing or thwarting takeovers, and hand out the necessary pink slips to employees. Research and development projects receive low priority.

Disgruntled bondholders are claiming foul play, and threaten, in the case of RJR Nabisco in a 1990 lawsuit against the firm, to require the refinancing of some $5 billion in outstanding RJR Nabisco debt. The claimants—Met Life, one of the nation's largest insurance companies, and Jefferson-Pilot, a small insurer based in Greensboro, NC, share the complaint of many investors of the result of a major buyout—that their investment grade debt is worth considerably less. Their suit contends that RJR violated "negative pledge covenants" that are routinely inserted as a protection in bond indentures—that a corporation issuing debt cannot pledge corporate assets to third parties or put liens on those assets without giving protection to existing bondholders. RJR, in order to pay off buyout-related bank debt in its $25 billion 1988 deal, pledged and ultimately sold off $6 billion in RJR assets. Complained one analyst of a company holding $18 million of RJR bonds, "We're sick and tired of takeovers . . . we bought a double A bond and now it's a double B. . . . That got pretty old fast" (*The New York Times,* May 20, 1990). This case is not unusual—junk bonds to finance buyouts in the merger rush defaulted or were slated to be swapped for securities of lower value at a record-breaking pace in 1989.

Why is it necessary to transfer to raiders billions of dollars of corporate assets in order to ensure management accountability? If management underutilizes a firm's resources, are takeover bids and leveraged buyouts an efficient, optimal way to regulate management? Or are there other forms of regulation that would redistribute the wealth to shareholders and society?

Regulation of management already exists: the Securities and Exchange Commission requires financial statement disclosures of publicly held companies, and an "attestation" (audit) by outside, independent accountants that the financial statements fairly present the financial position of the company according to generally accepted accounting principles (GAAP).

What, then, is going wrong? It seems prudent to ask: Why is the SEC and the accounting regulatory body, the Financial Accounting Standards Board (FASB), with yearly operating expenses of some $10 million, unable to ensure management accountability, i.e., stewardship to shareholders? Is it reasonable to expect the accounting profession to protect shareholders against management ineptitude? The SEC has granted the accounting profession considerable autonomy in the financial standard-setting process. Has this policy proved beneficial in light of these recent experiences?[1]

The notion that takeover bids and buyouts are a welcomed injection of democratic regulation in the marketplace raises doubts about the protection of shareholder interests afforded by the accounting profession. Viewing raiders as protectors of, and watchdogs for shareholders, contradicts the frequently promoted image that the profession advocates: that the essence of the profession is to "protect third-party interests," and that public accountants are public servants.

The passage of the Securities Act in 1933, many accountants claim, immersed the profession in the important role of holding management accountable to their shareholders. The takeover events demonstrate the strategic failure of the profession to respond to this challenge: to pioneer creative and innovative regulatory practices for advancing shareholder interests and promoting economic efficiency (for example, by devising reporting practices that highlight management efficiency and inefficiency). Why has accounting not pursued these goals? Is the accountant a third-party protector, i.e., a servant of shareholders and the public? Whose interests have been served by the role of accounting, and could there be other roles?

The reasons why the profession has not responded to challenges such as those presented above lie in understanding the kinds of social conflicts and pressures that the profession is subject to, i.e., why accounting practices and theories are a contested terrain. However, there have been few systematic studies of the origins and processes of social discord in accounting research. Most conventional accounting research omits and bypasses these considerations. Two questions are raised in this regard. First, what is the nature of social conflict in society (which requires a historical and social study)? Second, what part does accounting play in social struggle? (Here we should eventually be able to explain the omission of conflict in accounting research.)

The objective here is to contribute to a research area that is fundamental to the profession's future role in society: what is accounting's role in mediating, or reconstituting discord and whose interests does (and should) the discipline advance? The research differs from conventional studies by using a socio-historical approach, taking social struggle as problematic, and by exploring accounting's social role by examining its literature.

In order to ascertain why controversy has been so neglected, Chapter II begins by reviewing a series of definitions of accounting that are offered in the accounting literature. The chapter illustrates that in a variety of definitions of accounting, conflict has been downplayed, denied, or avoided. Without a framework of social discord, the profession remains impotent in comprehending its own struggles, as well as those embroiling shareholders, speculators, and other social constituencies.

Criteria for guiding accounting research are explored in Chapter III in terms of various epistemological positions. Here we see how inadequate epistemological arguments of the past permitted social conflict to be omitted from the accounting research agenda. In order to conceptualize the role of accounting in a context of social disputes, a new epistemological criterion is needed.

Chapter IV provides an in-depth examination of the nature of societal discords and ruptures and reveals many of the forces that shape and direct accounting practice under different social regimes. Accounting is viewed not merely as a disinterested recorder of affairs but as an active force in resolving the distribution of social wealth and income.

The literature review is presented in Chapter V. The study is an analysis of accounting and business journals during the period of 1960 through 1973. Classifying the literature enumerates accounting's participation in a variety of social disputes and contexts, exploring the changes in the literature (discourses) within that period. This discursive analysis shows that during this period accounting assumed a unique and distinctive role in mediating and displacing conflicts over the distribution of income and wealth. The specific ways in which accounting discharged this role varied from era to era, depending on the broader strategy of conflict management adopted by the state. Thus, when the state seeks to resolve conflict by arbitration and consensus, the accounting profession pursues one kind of mediation role, its discourse reflecting the benevolence of economic growth and the social benefits of a cooperative market place. When the state pursues a populist, authoritarian stance (exemplified by Margaret Thatcher in the United Kingdom and Ronald Reagan in the United States), the profession adopts quite a different posture: it insists that social regulation is best determined by a centralized authority—the profession's own institutions.

The book concludes with Chapter VI, Signs and Symbols: Rediscovering Accounting's Partisanship. The results of the study challenge an image of the profession as an objective, neutral observer. Rather, its protagonist character in privileging certain interests is explored: as part of the state apparatus in mediating conflict and in its ideological position, the profession participates in disputes over social wealth. These are not abstract conclusions, they are evidenced in social discords displayed, most recently, in hostile takeover battles, escalating thrift insolvencies, Third World debt moratoria, and commercial bailouts. They underscore the fact that accountants inevitably

choose sides in social affairs, and if such partisanship is unavoidable, then the profession needs a way to decide whose side
it will take. As the profession undergoes a congressional investigation for failing its public mandate in a number of financial
debacles, it seems at this juncture that the profession is already
being asked at high political levels whose side it is on.

Notes

1. The profits earned on takeover bids, the budget of the Securities and Exchange Commission, and the expenditures of the Financial Accounting Standards Board are not intended to represent comprehensive transaction costs of regulating management; rather, they illustrate a few possible components (among many) of the cost to society of regulating management.

CHAPTER II

THE ROLES OF ACCOUNTING IN SOCIETY

Accounting's failure to protect third party interests has been reflected most recently in savings and loans debacles, junk bond collapses, merger mania, government housing scandals, and Defense Department improprieties, but the question "to what degree are accountants responsible for the interests of shareholders, the public, and others?" has long plagued the profession. Ambiguities over accounting's allegiances are hardly new; rather they compose fundamental and unresolved controversies in the discipline. For example, accounting's "independence" is compromised and conflicts of interest emerge when accountants are hired by the very managers whose reports they must verify. Reporting the "facts" and "taking account" inevitably enhances the interests of some groups over others: Shareholders' interests versus managements', debt holder versus supplier, banker versus homeowner, accountant versus chief executive officer, and environmentalist versus engineer. The dilemma sometimes appears in an "equity versus efficiency" debate: Should the primary concern of the accounting professional be focused on equity issues and social welfare, or is the role of accounting to achieve efficiency, with equity a residual and subsidiary effect—tolerated, achieved by chance, but never actively pursued?

A tradition of accounting literature ignores the influence of accounting in social conflict and controversies, leaving the profession open to challenges of inconsistency and partisanship. Although the discipline is the target of criticism by managers, shareholders, bankers, state regulators, industry lobbyists, and labor unions, many accounting theorists hold fast to a memory of accounting as neutral, outside of political and social disputes. Having failed to recognize the significance of conflict, these researchers underestimate accounting practice, education, and theory as a contested terrain. The following section, by studying the genesis of accounting and analyzing its theoretical allegiances and affiliations, provides us with an assessment of its role in social conflict and its future.

The Stewardship Role

During the turbulent "trust and bust" period of the 1890s, stewardship accounting was advocated as the professional role for accountants. With the emergence, proliferation, and strengthening of the corporate form of business, the aim of holding management accountable to the "true" owners of the firm increased significantly. Events during this period offer insights into the interrelationship between the profession and its purposes, revealing ethical dilemmas and breakdowns of trust. Littleton and Zimmerman (1962) contend, "When management began to use capital other than its own, the possibility of human weakness in the face of temptation was certainly recognized" (p. 104). As the separation of ownership and control increased under the corporate form of enterprise, this type of organization posed new conflicts.

The involvement of bankers and outside promoters in the operations of U.S. corporations exacerbated concern that promoters and financiers were "interested in profits to be made from issuing securities [i.e., speculation] and powers to be gained in arranging mergers and acquisitions" (Clews, in Previts and Merino, 1979, p. 129). Suggestions were made by the president of the New York Stock Exchange, economists, state regulators, and others that public disclosure of corporate activities would be an effective means of preventing and combating speculation abuse and fraud. Accounting's significance in this process strengthened, as evidenced by the following suggestion by the Industrial Commission of the U.S. Senate,[1] in 1900, that "an independent public accounting profession ought to be established if corporate abuses . . . were to be curtailed effectively" (Previts and Merino, 1979, p. 133).

Management's stewardship could not be assumed; rather "audit actions were no doubt devised in the belief that the scrutiny of a person's report of the discharge of his responsibilities was beneficial both for him and for the interests he served" (Littleton and Zimmerman, 1962, p. 104). That such scrutiny of accountability should be made by third parties engenders the basic idea of an independent audit (Hatfield, 1909; May, 1936; Paton, 1922; and Scott, 1931). As a "tool for guaranteeing that management appropriately fulfill its stewardship function towards its stockholders" (Ronen, 1979, p. 415), accounting's social usefulness and import was established.

Statements by the American Institute of Certified Public Accountants (AICPA) Study Group of Objectives (1973) confirm the profession's emphasis on stewardship and the significance attached to that role. Noting that "Reporting on management's stewardship has long been recognized as a principal purpose of financial statements" (p. 25), accounting's role in reporting to outside owners of corporations—its third party responsibility—has been dominant throughout accounting history. The contribution (or potential contribution) of accounting in protecting stockholders and others against managerial manipulation has been discussed in the accounting literature for well over six decades (e.g., Briloff, 1981; Canning, 1929; Chatfield, 1978; Hatfield, 1909; Kohler, 1940; May, 1936; Paton, 1922; Scott, 1931; and Spacek, 1964).

Yet not everyone views accounting as a protective shield for outsiders in evaluating management's stewardship role. Hurst (1970) provides evidence that accounting served to rationalize and justify the corporate entity in the early 1900s, by not merely describing effective management, but legitimizing corporate power and maintaining confidence. The "really effective pressures for shareholder information grew out of concern for maintaining confidence in the market for corporate securities, rather than for the legitimacy of the internal government of the corporation" (p. 91). In effect, asserts Hurst, twentieth century state and federal law accepted corporations in such sizes and shapes as business people could develop them. Utilizing disclosure rules as a means of effecting some monitoring over corporations, legislation was in fact reflecting continuing acceptance of substantial corporate autonomy, rather having the primary purpose of controlling corporate power (Merino and Neimark, 1982).

The New Stewardship Role:
The Efficient Allocation of Resources

The 1973 report on the objectives of financial statements by the American Institute of Certified Public Accountants (AICPA) provides an "economic" rather than merely "legalistic" definition of stewardship: "Stewardship refers to the efficient administration of resources and the execution of plans for conserving and consuming them" (p. 25). Chen (1975) has suggested that this report can be interpreted as expressing "a higher form of stewardship—an accounting for effective use not merely for custody or maintenance" (see Chen, 1975, p. 533).

Although the traditional stewardship role is still important, the AICPA recognizes that the performance of management is not easily assessed through financial reporting of the enterprise's performance. In order to assist users, suggests the Institute, managers should report expectations, disclose assumptions, and differentiate between factual and interpretive information. This information will assist users in evaluating management's performance apart from the firm (AICPA, 1973, 1974).

Such statements contrast with the aim of maintenance or safeguarding of these resources, implying that stewardship and the reporting of stewardship should be redefined as the effective utilization of a firm's resources. Benston (1982a, 1982b) also suggests distinctions between corporate accountability (stewardship) and disclosure informativeness (effective utilization). Citing the U.S. Securities Act of 1933 and the U.S. Securities Exchange Act of 1934, he maintains that managements "were supposed to provide investors with [1] reports of stewardship and [2] with economic information so that they could make informed decisions" (Benston, 1982a, p. 87).

A question arises: why distinguish between these functions of accounting? Are the distinctions superfluous? It would seem that accounting reports on management's fulfillment of their responsibility to outside owners (the old stewardship notion) would have always necessitated considering management's effectiveness and efficiency (the new informativeness role).

Nevertheless, accounting's role in informativeness and efficiency, in a social context, has been increasingly emphasized by the profession. The AICPA frames these relationships in the following way:

> Financial statements are often audited by independent accountants for the purpose of enhancing confidence in their reliability. . . . Well developed securities markets tend to allocate scarce resources to enterprises that use them efficiently and away from enterprises that use them inefficiently. . . . Financial reporting is intended to provide information that is useful in making reasoned choices among alternative uses of scarce resources in the conduct of business activities (AICPA, 1973, pp. 13–26).

These views, reiterated by FASB pronouncement (1978), have formed the basis of accounting objectives, practices, standards, and principles into the 1990s. As is apparent from these statements, the informational role of accounting is regarded as a crucial link in the efficient allocation of society's resources by individuals, enterprises, and government. The recent emphasis on the role of accounting in the efficient allocation of resources has been classified under the user-informativeness approach, (see Benston, 1982a, 1982b; Chambers, 1966; Edwards and Bell, 1961; FASB, 1978; Gonedes and Dopuch, 1974; AICPA, 1973; Ronen, 1979; and Sterling, 1974) or agency theory (see De Angelo, 1988; Jensen and Meckling, 1976; Ronen, 1979; and Watts and Zimmerman, 1978, 1979, 1990). Positive accounting theory—that brand of research calling for the study of "what is," in contrast to what should be—also emerged as a research program in the 1970s, as we shall describe later.

A distinctly different history from this chronology of accounting's past is reflected in current critical accounting literature. Characteristic of this literature is a scrutiny of precepts that accounting is informationally useful in a neutral way, or that accounting ensures efficiency in a market economy. These studies explore: the interpretive, hermeneutic, and discursive role of accounting (Arrington and Francis, 1989a; Chua, 1988; and Lehman and Tinker, 1987), accounting's professional myth making and control practices (Armstrong, 1985, 1987; Boland, 1982; Cooper, 1980a, 1980b; and Gallhofer and Haslam, 1991); accounting's creation of reality in communicating reality (Hines, 1988a, 1988b, 1989; Hopwood, 1985; Okcabol and Tinker, 1990; and Tinker et al., 1982); critical histories of accounting (Hopper et al., 1986 and Loft, 1986); accounting's role in crafting selves and as a source of disciplinary power and knowledge (Hoskin and Macve, 1986; Knights and Collinson, 1987; Knights and Willmott, 1985); and the disruptive role of accounting in social conflict (Neimark, 1983; Tinker et al., 1988). These incursions into the history of accounting depart from convention by rejecting objectivity and the search for ultimate truth; rather they privilege the shaping of shared subjectivities.

Returning back to the review of the traditional lineage of accounting, several questions emerge: what is the relationship between information to investors and the efficient allocation of resources in society? If accounting provides the information, will, as many researchers claim, market forces complete the cycle and establish the efficient allocation of resources? How do assumptions about society, which guide these theories, affect the perceived role of accounting and ultimately accounting's role in social conflict? These issues are addressed next.

The Efficient Allocation of Resources: General Characteristics, Limitations, and Challenges

The AICPA (1973, 1974), the FASB (1978), and numerous researchers contend that accounting performs a useful function by serving the needs of investors.[2] The usefulness of accounting stems from a belief that if accounting could provide information aiding investors in allocating their wealth, the marketplace would function efficiently, ensuring maximum social welfare.

One limitation of this view is its focus on shareholders (both potential and current). Shareholders' heterogeneous interests are not necessarily representative of the heterogeneous interests of all social members. Thus, maximization of shareholder investment wealth does not guarantee an adequate criterion for societal wealth (financial or non-financial).

Additional problems arise: how should investor utility be measured? Numerous accounting researchers assume stock price maximization is a measure of shareholder utility maximization. But how can we justify using stock price as a measure of well-offness of the individual investor and for investors as a group? Fama and Miller (1972) illustrate the weakness of such approaches. They contend that for the rule of shareholder wealth to have unambiguous meaning (i.e., to establish a measure of investor wealth as a group) it would require a world of homogeneous investor expectations (p. 301).[3] In addition, for share prices (market values) to serve as a proxy for individual shareholder utility, assumptions of perfect capital markets are required (p. 76).[4]

The assertion that accounting serves society by serving stockholders in the aggregate is compromised by the results above. More fundamental problems with this view, because of its reliance on neo-classical economics, have been observed in the literature as well (Sraffa, 1960; Chua, 1986; Cooper, 1980a, 1980b; Hines, 1988b; Lowe et al., 1983; Okcabol, 1989; and Tinker, 1980, 1984). Conventional accounting research relies extensively upon the neo-classical economic model (explicitly or implicitly), thus, the remaining sections of this chapter examine the difficulties that this poses for accounting.

Assumptions of Neo-Classical Economics and Their Impact on Accounting

The neo-classical model has been criticized because of:

(1) its assumptions concerning the marketplace;
(2) the generalization of individual preferences to collective preferences;
(3) the separation of social and economic spheres for analysis.[5]

Assumptions Concerning the Marketplace

Researchers frequently begin their work by assuming markets are competitive, yet quickly restructure that assumption because they recognize that perfect competition rarely exists. Admitting the prevalence of "breakdowns" in competitive markets, they assert that sufficient adjustments take place, rectifying divergences from pure competition. Contending that market mechanisms will correct any dysfunctional behavior among market transactors (particularly any behavior that may be dysfunctional to investors, customers, etc.), for these researchers Adam Smith's invisible hand may be visible, but the results are the same—the marketplace "works" (i.e., it ensures markets produce and distribute goods and services in an optimal manner;

cf. Marshall, 1920, p. 333; Cohen and Cyert, 1975, pp. 49–51). Yet numerous studies indicate that oligopolistic, monopolistic, monopsonistic, and other non-purely competitive situations are prevalent in the marketplace (Baran and Sweezy, 1966; Galbraith, 1954; Hirschleifer, 1971; and Samuelson, 1984).

Graaf (1975) has demonstrated that the attempt to aggregate the workings of a competitive free market in order to produce optimal economic efficiency requires at least seventeen assumptions. He suggests it is "astonishing" that professional economists have worked for so long with a neo-classical framework (Cooper, 1980a, 1980b; and Katouzian, 1980). Current research suggests that divergences from competition are significant and that market mechanisms cannot be relied upon, on their own, to efficiently allocate resources.

Two competing theories about market forces that have emerged in accounting research are presented below. One school of thought asserts that accounting lacks real social significance because market mechanisms provide sufficient incentives for disclosure without "onerous" accounting regulation (onerous in a number of ways: e.g., it is costly in that it uses resources to produce the information, and disclosure could lessen natural market incentives for production, invention, etc. [these issues are explored in Hirschleifer, 1971; Fama and Laffer, 1971; Marshall, 1974; and Ronen, 1977]). A second, competing, view justifies the existence of accounting for the very reason that many of the assumptions of perfect competition do not hold. For example, perfect competition assumes transactors have equal access to all information, including states of the world—assumptions that do not hold. This existence of information asymmetry is one reason accounting is crucial in the market-place, providing public access to previously private, inside information, and assisting in the efficient allocation of resources.

Below we present the first view, that accounting interferes with market forces, and is inefficient in the allocation of resources (i.e., "markets are better than accounting"). We then describe the second view, which challenges the claim that market forces are better than accounting regulations. Exploring this controversy will help explicate our primary concern: reconstructing the role of accounting in society.

"Markets Are Better Than Accounting"

Benston's research[6] challenges the view that accounting disclosure requirements serve a useful function for shareholders and/or society. Benston contends that although corporate managers have the discretion to use shareholders' resources in ways that are detrimental to shareholder interests, managers are constrained from doing so. For Benston, managers act on behalf of shareholder interests (the maximization of shareholder wealth) because of incentives and restrictions in the market-place.

Four factors constrain managers from diverging from shareholder interest (Benston, 1982a). First, in markets for the firm's goods and services, customers have sufficient alternatives and discretion, even in monopolized industries, to ensure that corporations provide what the customers want. Benston links this (customer) market pressure and management's concern for shareholder wealth maximization as follows: adverse customer behavior is a discipline upon management behavior because management's rewards may depend on their position as shareholders in the company.

Benston's second limitation is that the markets for finance and for corporate control also constrain managerial behavior to be consistent with the maximization of shareholder wealth. He suggests, for example, that poor stewardship can result in higher borrowing rates which decreases the manager's wealth (as a shareholder), and increases the likelihood that managers will be displaced through takeovers of poorly managed (and low valued) companies.

The market for managerial services is a third restriction on managerial discretion. As is the case with markets generally, the market for executives is deemed competitive. Executives, seeking to enhance their market value by establishing a good track record, recognize that poor or self-serving decisions will damage their value to their consumers, i.e., shareholders.

The last constraint on management arises from internal and external monitoring systems. Internal monitoring is in the manager's self-interest because the manager's own rewards depend on the performance of others; thus managers will police each other. External monitoring reports are sought by management because without such monitoring, shareholders would reduce management compensation by the amount shareholders expect the managers will divert from the company. This is the argument of Jensen and Meckling's work (1976) in their formulation of agency theory (i.e., managers as agents of shareholders). They argue that, in most cases, managers bear all agency costs,[7] and thus, managers would voluntarily supply the information necessary to monitor their own performance.

Benston, as well as Jensen and Meckling, acknowledged limitations on the usefulness of accounting in constraining management behavior. For example, Benston notes that although accounting standards have been advocated as a means of advancing the interests of shareholders and/or society, these standards are unlikely to do so (Benston, 1982b, p. 5). Thus, he favors limiting the amount of regulation of accounting standard setting.

Benston's belief in managerial constraint through the markets for finance, managerial services, and products ensures that they act in the interests of shareholders. Thus accounting standards have no special role to play in corporate governance and social responsibility. Furthermore, agency theory supports the expectation that corporate managers will voluntarily tend to publish accounting data that maximize the wealth of the shareholders. He concludes, "Shareholders will be hurt if externally determined accounting standards are imposed on the managers" (Benston, 1982b, p. 9).

Benston's criticism of regulation is broader than just accounting standards. In his study of the SEC Act of 1934, he concludes, "There appears to have been little basis for the legislation and no evidence that it was needed or desirable. Certainly there is doubt that more required disclosure is warranted" (1967, p. 153). A similar call for limiting disclosure standards and regulations has been made by Sunder (1981), who suggests that instead of trying to distinguish between good and bad research, and good and bad accounting methods, and, given the enormous proliferation of FASB rules and standards, the FASB should codify as standards only those accounting practices that have been popular with and are accepted by business people as a result of the free play of market forces. In other words, the information that should be disclosed should be the information management would disclose without the pressure of external accounting standards.

Watts and Zimmerman's research (1978, 1979, 1990) challenges the role of accounting, and in particular, the purpose and usefulness of accounting theories. Accounting theories have the characteristics of goods in a marketplace; therefore, they are demanded by managers and accounting policy makers in order to justify their views. The most desirable theories, suggest Watts and Zimmerman, are those that appeal to the public interest because self-interests can be hidden under the guise of serving the public. Watts and Zimmerman conclude that there will never be any comprehensive accounting theory because accounting theories are excuses demanded and negotiated for in the marketplace of theories. For Watts and Zimmerman, accounting theories are apologies: managers use them to rationalize their behavior. Instead, Watts and Zimmerman advocate a return to the free play of market forces where the reports and standards that management provides, and adheres to, emerge without "the" accounting theory. The implication of Watts and Zimmerman's research, as with the others above, is that the marketplace would be more efficient without a state regulatory interference, i.e., accounting.[8, 9]

In summary, the above researchers support market regulations over governmental and accounting regulation, utilizing efficient market theories or agency theory as a justification. Agency theory, concerned with contracting and bonding between owners (shareholders) and their agents (management), contends that the optimal arrangement, minimizing agents' costs, occurs through market mechanisms. Efficient market research also suggests that an optimal allocation of resources is obtainable through market forces (Gonedes and Dopuch, 1974; Beaver, 1974; and Dukes, 1975).

That management is monitored through natural market forces, not politico-regulatory mandate, has been challenged by a number of researchers. One response to the proposition is to demonstrate that agency costs are not borne by the managers, i.e., that the managers' self-interests are not sufficient to protect the shareholders' interests. We will illustrate this analysis of agency theory using research by Ronen (1979) because it provides a comprehensive challenge to researchers such as Benston, Jensen and Meckling, and Watts and Zimmerman. However, Ronen's analysis is incomplete, as we shall see; placed within a neo-classical framework, he fails to problematize accounting's pivotal role in resource allocation as a subjective, politically imbued practice, and not a neutral social position.

Critique of "Markets are Better Than Accounting"

Ronen recognizes that one characteristic of an agency relationship is the potential for managers to be motivated to promote their self-interests. Managers may be motivated to take a chance and try to promote poor quality securities—analogous to selling a used car that is a lemon. Managers with a high taste for non-pecuniary benefits will have an incentive to bias information to potential investors (because the financial return from securities accrues to all shareholders, and it usually forms only a small part of the manager's income). At the same time, managers of quality firms will be trying to establish their quality and will use some market mechanism to do so.

Providing information to shareholders, for example, in financial reports is akin to advertisement; it is one mechanism for managers to promote their companies. Yet the problem of information asymmetry exists in that shareholders do not know which financial reports are representative of management's true consumption of non-pecuniary benefits. Information asymmetry in this context is management's knowledge of his or her taste for non-pecuniary benefits, and investors' lack of this knowledge, and inability to gain access to that information.

Here, states Ronen, accounting steps in to provide assurances. The audit of financial statements and the application of uniform standards in the preparation of these statements is "a social arrangement that facilitates the kind of monitoring that reduces uncertainty [and ambiguity] of [erroneous] inferences at minimal costs" (Ronen, 1979, p. 426). One disadvantage of this arrangement, for Ronen, is the reduction of management's flexibility in signaling to investors. However, "as in most economic activities . . . there is an optimal amount of uniformity of accounting standards, an optimum that balances the costs of limiting management's flexibility and signalling against the benefits inherent in the reduction of monitoring costs due to uniformity" (Ronen, 1979, p. 426). Within the marketplace the pricing mechanism is intended to distinguish good management from poor management, which might be achieved with the information that management provides on a voluntary basis. However, assurances that this information is correct cannot come, according to Ronen, from the marketplace.

In defense of accounting regulation, Ronen disagrees that there exist sufficient incentives in the market system for a firm's management, operating in its self-interest, to be optimally accountable and informative. He contends that regulation might be, and probably is, necessary as an efficient way of dealing with the problems of agency costs under conditions of information asymmetry (i.e., management has information that investors do not have). In addition, Ronen believes that the role of informativeness for accounting is not a false rationalization or an excuse to justify governmental regulation, as suggested by Watts and Zimmerman. Accounting offers the opportunity for management to signal quality performance (non-lemons); regulation of this signaling emerges from the problem of information asymmetry. Accounting is a crucial link in the chain of processes leading to efficient resource allocation.

Ronen, in contrast to Benston, Watts and Zimmerman, and others, demonstrates that market forces (*ex* accounting) do not automatically result in the efficient allocation of resources. Although Ronen's well-developed critique comprehensively discredits these researchers, his challenge, based on economic analysis, recommends a corrective *market* mechanism for resolving information asymmetry. Unfortunately, his notion of information asymmetry does not extend to an examination of the social relationships underlying information asymmetry, and more generally, asymmetry in the distribution of economic power (e.g., property rights). Ronen's analysis leaves unanswered important questions concerning the relationship between efficiency and equity, or more specifically, efficiency and distribution. This relationship, fundamental to understanding the politico-economic and social roles of accounting, is explored next.

Summary of Assumptions Concerning the Marketplace

Although researchers disagree to what extent accounting contributes to the efficient allocation of resources, we have observed that in many cases much research of this genre is based on similar theoretical assumptions. Implicitly and explicitly, these frameworks frequently depend on neo-classical economic theory. Yet a neo-classical framework results in inconsistencies and problematic implications concerning the role of accounting. Three limitations, in particular, have not been adequately addressed by these accounting researchers.

First, assumptions concerning the marketplace led Ronen to conclude that accounting regulations and standards were justified. The other two limitations, which were not resolved by Ronen's critique, are the aggregation of individual preferences to obtain collective preferences and the separation of the social and economic spheres for analysis. We turn to these issues next, and to their implications for accounting's role.

Aggregating Individual Preferences to Obtain Social Welfare

Accounting researchers suggest that the efficient allocation of resources in society is advanced by accounting through the interaction of investors in capital markets. In formulating a conceptual framework of accounting, the FASB argues that the decisions of investors and creditors significantly affect the allocation of resources in the economy (FASB "Statement of Financial Accounting Concepts No. 1: Objectives of Financial Reporting of Business Enterprises," 1978, p. 14).

Many of the previously cited studies analyze the role of accounting in the efficient allocation of resources by studying stockholder preferences and analyzing changes in security prices. The prevalence of this research is illustrated in numerous accounting studies under the domain of "Efficient Market Hypothesis" research, which focuses on the effect of accounting information on securities prices (see Dyckman et al., 1975; Watts and Zimmerman, 1990).[10] Within an efficient markets framework, information provided by accountants often contributes to a better functioning of capital markets (Dyckman et al., 1975 p. xii). The role of information, viewed as central to setting the relative securities price structure, plays a vital role in the allocation of resources among firms and securities among individuals (p. 78). Characteristically, these studies analyze the role of accounting in the efficient allocation of resources by assessing stockholders' preferences. Although stockholders have heterogeneous interests, researchers analyzing individual preferences assume an additive nature, conducting the analysis as if preferences or utility, once they are aggregated, constitute a society's collective preferences.[11, 12]

Neo-classical analysis typically resolves social choice questions by adopting an individualistic orientation and assuming that individual utilities can be aggregated and compared. Yet classical political economists (cf. Dobb, 1937, and more recently, Arrow, 1971) have demonstrated the impossibility of using individuals' utility functions for analysis of collective utility for a society. Arrow, questioning how a model for society can be generalized for more than one individual if utility functions cannot be compared, concludes that social choices, affecting more than one individual, can only be made by a dictator. Beaver and Demski (1974), Gonedes and Dopuch (1974), and Ronen and Sorter (1978) regard this as a dilemma for accounting—the selection among accounting alternatives is a "problem of social choice" (Ronen and Sorter, 1978, p. 1). Concluding that we cannot avoid the dictatorial conclusions of Arrow at the present time, Demski (1974) asserts "the question of what we mean by an optimal set of financial reporting systems cannot be approached by assimilating [aggregating] individual preferences and opinions" (p. 228).

Ronen and Sorter disagree with this conclusion. They see the accounting profession as able to assist in the allocation of resources. Accounting researchers (including Beaver and Demski, Gonedes and Dopuch, and Ronen and Sorter) recognize that the choice among reporting alternatives has social consequences that affect non-users and users of accounting information. The primary effect of interest here is in terms of the distribution of wealth among social members. Accepting Arrow's conclusions, Beaver and Demski argue that in order to choose among accounting alternatives, ethical judgements must be made as to whose well-being should be enhanced and whose should be diminished.

The above analysis implies we cannot recommend optimal accounting alternatives unless: (1) we act in a dictatorial fashion; (2) we commit ourselves to making value judgements; and (3) we abandon our assumption that stockholders' utility is useful in assessing the role of accounting in efficient resource allocation. For Beaver, Demski, Gonedes, and Dopuch, accountants should continue to search for the accounting alternatives that individuals prefer. In other words, accounting should search for a mapping of individual preference orderings over accounting alternatives.

Individual preference orderings are useful in choosing optimal reporting decisions when researchers adopt a Pareto optimality criterion, which occurs when the selection of a choice alternative (compared with the status quo) makes at least one individual better off, but no one else worse off. Accounting researchers, arguing that as long as one individual is better off and no individual is worse off in terms of a current distribution of resources, accept the criterion of Pareto optimal distribution, ignoring that this formulation relies entirely on individuals' preferences and is only weakly generalized to a social preference function. The implication is highly conservative in that the status quo rules unless it can be bettered, displacing value judgments in choosing the initial status quo. Accounting researchers use the criterion of Pareto optimality as a neutral, objective, or non-ethical decision criterion, yet it implicitly assumes the current distribution is somehow superior. However, there is nothing distinctive about wealth distribution associated with the status quo; indeed, for some social members, it will be an unacceptable state of affairs—not a neutral benchmark of distribution. A Pareto optimal criterion ignores the role of social structure in creating inequality between social members. Culture, prejudice, institutions, and heredity restrict access to wealth quite independently of a social member's performance in the marketplace (see Katouzian, 1980; and Lindblom, 1982).

Ronen and Sorter reject Beaver and Demski's conclusions, that the social choice problem must be resolved by attempting to define individuals' preference orderings over accounting alternatives. Ronen and Sorter (1978) argue that the social choice problem should be decomposed into two stages: (1) choices that should be made by accountants regarding the accounting alternatives that maximize the efficient allocation of resources ("defining the desired accounting alternatives that maximize aggregate monetary wealth over all" [p. 2]) and (2) the political or equity choices to be made by government regulators, etc., as to how to distribute resources.

In Ronen and Sorter's opinion, this framework frees accounting regulators and standard setters from making value judgements and subjective decisions. In their words, this separation of the choice problem into wealth maximization and socially desirable wealth distribution would allow accounting regulators to specify accounting rules and procedures whose objective is efficient resource allocation. It would also allow social and political scientists to adopt compensation schemes to reallocate the resulting wealth among individuals and groups in society in a socially desirable manner (Ronen and Sorter, 1978, p. 2).

The Separation of Social and Economic Spheres

The above solution raises a number of difficult questions. For example, is accounting objective if it maximizes wealth but ignores the social desirability of various distributions of wealth? Can such separations be made, and why are these theoretically and practically desirable distinctions? In previous research, Ronen discusses the importance of the new role of accounting in informativeness and in efficient allocation of resources, and thus "accounting information should serve ultimately to enhance social welfare" (1979, p. 432). How can accounting enhance social welfare on the one hand and claim that it is inappropriate for accounting to consider the distribution of resources of income and wealth on the other? Ronen leaves us with no justification for separating economic issues and political and social issues in the search for an enhancement of social welfare.

Similar questions can be directed against Benston, who argues that economic values are "necessarily subjectively determined" (1982a, p. 102), and thus cannot be included in audited reports.[13] In Benston's view accounting should confine itself to the concern for "recording, presenting and auditing market transactions. . . . Despite the desires of many for reports of economic values . . . the amounts are too ambiguous to be included in reports which a public accountant attests to" (p. 102). Again, it is assumed that market transactions are separate from activities which are subjective, or socially determined. But market values, determined within a particular environment which is itself an array of social relationships and social values, are inevitably socially constituted. The dynamic interaction of numerous factors, including social values affecting market transactions and prices, surely refutes the claim that accounting is value free.

Neo-classical assertions that the initial distribution of wealth and power in society can be dealt with independently from production and exchange problems is naively accepted by these researchers. Yet even as early as Adam Smith, economists recognized that (income) distribution and production decisions were inseparable. For Marshall, they were like blades of a pair of scissors where movement in one blade automatically changed the relative position of the other blade.

More recently, Sraffa (1960) has shown that it is not logically possible to develop production conditions independent of distribution conditions. Ultimately, the optimum rate of interest (to the production factor, capital) is socially determined, and can only be derived by assuming a specific distribution of wealth (Cooper, 1980a, 1980b; Tinker, 1980). "Different distributions of wealth imply differing rates of interest and hence differing production conditions" (Cooper, 1980a, 1980b). A number of researchers have demonstrated that the neo-classical model, in seeking to ignore income and wealth distribution, becomes a tautology (e.g., Robinson, 1953–1954; Harcourt, 1969; and Samuelson, 1966). They illustrate that neo-classical theory— marginal productivity theory—is indeterminate, because in order to explain how the optimal vector of factor input prices for an economy is determined, one needs to assume a given distribution of income, which is what the model is supposed to explain! Specifically, in order to derive the rate of profit, i.e., the returns to capital, researchers use the market rate of interest to find the capital stock. But it is this profit rate the marginal theory is supposed to determine.

The spurious separation of production from distribution by neo-classical theorists has been noted by numerous researchers. Harcourt (1969), who reviews what has become known as the Cambridge controversies, states that, "the theory of production relations was meant to be independent of the institutions of society; that is, relations between men were treated as irrelevant for an explanation of distribution . . . this separation is invalid, even in the world of pure logic, and the significance of this distinction for the case of more than one capital good has been emphasized by the modern critics of the neoclassical parables" (p. 395).

Summary and Challenges

Orthodox accounting researchers such as Ronen claim that accounting has an important role to play in enhancing social welfare, and that this role should be researched within an economic framework. However, the neo-classical economic framework looks toward maximizing overall wealth and leaves questions concerning the distribution of this wealth completely unresolved. By separating the analysis into economic or social frameworks, attention is diverted away from the value judgements that accountants inevitably commit by relying on the choices of others.

In "Concepts No. 1" (1978), the FASB emphasizes the importance of accounting in the efficient allocation of resources. The AICPA report, *Objectives of Financial Statements*, states, "While the means of achieving allocation of resources in the economy are subject to debate, probably none would question the desirability of efficient allocation as a goal. As to equity criteria relative to the distribution of wealth, they are clearly implicit objectives" (AICPA, 1973, p. 38, ft. 5). These views continue to be an integral basis of the formation of accounting pronouncements, standards, rules, and practice.

With accounting practice and research granting efficiency primary importance, equity has been relegated to a secondary status. Remarks that equity is an implicit objective is a mystification, because in the pursuit of efficiency, researchers completely ignore issues concerning equity. The various ways in which these trade-offs and intellectual sleights of hand are accomplished include placing the equity decision in the hands of politicians, assuming the status quo is Pareto optimal, and assuming that accounting is objective and unbiased toward the interests of certain groups. In each case, the solution is achieved largely by ignoring the problem.

In response to these inadequacies, accounting research has more recently developed alternative explanations and theories of accounting's roles. Under the rubric of critical, radical, social, and interpretive accounting, these theories recognize the broad ideological and subjective nature of the practice. Critically examining the political and social spheres that accounting affects, this research examines the profession's role in creating governable persons through disciplinary power (Hoskin and Macve, 1986; Knights, 1985; Knights and Collinson, 1987; and Miller and O'Leary, 1987); in perpetuating the status quo (Burchell et al., 1980; Hopper et al., 1986, 1987; Hopwood, 1984; Lowe et al., 1983; Knights and Willmott, 1985; and Merino and Neimark, 1982); as partisan in social conflicts (Armstrong, 1985; Chua, 1986; Cooper, 1981, 1984; Hoogvelt and Tinker, 1978; Loft, 1986; Neimark, 1990; Okcabol and Tinker, 1990; and Tinker, 1985); in formulating ethical practices (Briloff, 1981, 1990; Lehman, 1988; and Parker, 1986), and as an ideological system for seeing the world (Arrington and Francis, 1989a, 1989b; Chua, 1988; Gallhofer and Haslam, 1991; Hines, 1988a, 1989; Laughlin, 1987; Lehman and Tinker, 1987; and Tinker et al., 1988).

Thus, there is within accounting research a literature recognizing the shifting and contested character of accounting practice that challenges the status quo. By illustrating how accounting helps constitute symbolic discourse and therefore co-determine the outcomes of social struggles, this research challenges those who denigrate the importance of accounting in shaping social affairs. Radical studies, rejecting pluralistic thinking, document the structural inequalities and disadvantages of contemporary capitalism, and the movement of capitalism from one crisis to the next. The enduring nature of the radical critique is attributable to the persistence of these underlying social antagonisms to which it attempts to speak, and to the complicity of accountants, which it seeks to elucidate.

The above discussion leads to two routes to better understanding the profession's role. One route approaches accounting in its social context, incorporating its environment and recognizing its social construction in a historical manner. By examining the cultural, economic, and political environment of accounting, we assess its social origins, its present and potential functions, its connection to the state apparatus, its role in social discord, and its effect on social beliefs.

A related concern emerges from the ambiguity surrounding accounting's role. Returning to the concern of the profession and the convention of some researchers regarding accounting objectivity, the question arises as to what criteria should be established for the development and assessment of research in accounting? These are the issues addressed in the next chapter. Issues regarding research criteria, inevitably imbued with social and historical affairs, will be subsequently assimilated into this broader perspective in Chapter IV.

Notes

1. The Industrial Commission was established in 1898 to investigate matters concerning immigration, labor, agriculture, manufacturing, and business (see Previts and Merino, 1979, pp. 133–135).

2. The AICPA and the FASB regard the needs of creditors, potential investors, consumers, etc., important as well, but regard the needs of investors as primary (AICPA, 1973; FASB, 1978).

3. A world of homogeneous investor expectations would require, for example, that they agree on probabilities of outcomes and states of nature, i.e., that their beliefs are the same when choosing among investments.

4. Assumptions of perfect capital markets would require, for example, that markets operate under competitive circumstances, with access to information equally available to all market participants, thus insuring that investors' preferences are converted into a marketplace price.

5. Additional critiques of neo-classical economics include: material wealth maximization equates with social wealth maximization and the analysis fails to capture externalities.

6. See Benston, 1967, 1973, 1979/1980, 1982a, 1982b.

7. Jensen and Meckling (1976) describe agency costs between a principal (owner) and the agent (who is engaged to perform a service on behalf of the principal) as the sum of: the monitoring expenditures by the principal, the bonding expenditures of the agent, and the residual loss (i.e., the divergency between the agent's decisions and those which would maximize the welfare of the principal) (p. 308).

8. See Lowe et al. (1983), who critique Watts and Zimmerman for their (unjustified) use of an economic framework to explain a political process, for their positivist approach, and for ambiguities that render their model impossible to test. See also Christenson, 1983.

9. Watts and Zimmerman's view of state regulations, which includes the bargaining for state favors, the capturing of state regulators, and the supply and demand for public interest theories relies on an underlying framework of the state associated with Stigler, 1971; Peltzman, 1976; and Posner, 1974. The controversies surrounding these views are discussed in greater detail in Chapter IV.

10. Dyckman et al., 1975, review this research, and point out the substantial amount of research done in this area, e.g., Ball and Brown, 1968; Beaver, 1972; Collins, 1975; Dukes, 1975; Fama et al., 1969; Gonedes, 1975; and Pattell, 1976.

11. Research has been conducted which adjusts for heterogeneous assumptions, e.g., Beaver, 1972; Levy, 1972; Rubenstein, 1975; and Stiglitz, 1972.

12. Dyckman et al., 1975, in their study of efficient markets and accounting, refer to the frequent appeal to Pareto optimality criteria as too simple a solution to ordinarily suffice.

13. An example of economic values would be the costs (or measure) of an externality such as pollution imposed upon the public by a corporation.

CHAPTER *III*

TRUTH OR CONSEQUENCES: THE SOCIAL PRODUCTION OF KNOWLEDGE

Every policy, strategy, or claim to truth implies, directly or indirectly, an epistemological position that authorizes or legitimizes the claim or policy advocated. Even in formulating accounting policy, the adoption of an epistemological position is unavoidable. Accordingly, rather than allow an epistemology to emerge unsystematically and without critical examination here, this chapter explores a number of fundamental issues relating to the research process in an attempt to set forth criteria for assessing research. What becomes apparent in the following review is that definitions of knowledge, discovery, truth, fact, or validity are problematic. By carefully considering the consequences of choosing particular standards for judging research, our understanding of knowledge production and the struggle over meaning is enriched.

Presenting the grounds of knowledge (epistemology) is a formidable task. What follows is a modest attempt to articulate the philosophical underpinnings needed to ground research in accounting. The initial sections review various epistemological stances and the controversies surrounding these views. This is followed by a discussion of epistemological controversies among accounting researchers. The final section introduces a particular framework to guide and assess research in a framework which suggests that accounting research such as that proposed in this book should view accounting within its historical and social context as a participant in social conflict.

Epistemological Stance: Falsificationism

In an attempt to establish criteria for assessing research, Popper concerned himself with questions such as: Does the research produce statements which can be justified or proven false or true? Is the research and theory objective? Is there a methodology to research that can be formulated to ensure that all research inquiry is value free and neutral? (Popper, 1965, p. 31; 1976, p. 96). Among his conclusions, Popper advocates that falsification is a methodology of conducting research that can advance knowledge and ensure, in the long run, objectivity. His reasonings are examined below.

Popper directed an important challenge to prevailing social science research by rejecting the inductive approach to social science research.[1] Under this method a researcher begins with observations and measurements, proceeds by induction to generalizations, and then formulates theories. Popper describes the attempt to conduct social science research in this inductive, naturalistic, scientific approach as a misguided attempt toward the "ideal of scientific objectivity" (Popper, 1976, p. 91).[2]

In an important rebuke to the received methodology, Popper rejected the suggestion that social and natural science researchers could ever be value free or objective, because all individuals were imbued with "the value system of his own social class" (1976, p. 90). However, Popper declares that although scientists are partisan and biased, it is a mistake to assume that the objectivity of a science depends upon the objectivity of individual scientists. He contends that the social or ideological habitat of the researcher "tends to be eliminated in the long run" (p. 96), a claim suggesting that it is possible to free science from involvement in value judgements. Ultimately, objective truth is attainable in Popper's view, through an accumulation of knowledge guided by a deductive theoretical and methodological approach to research (Popper, 1957).

Popper claims that value freedom is attainable by differentiating between purely scientific values and extra-scientific values. The former concerns, for example, the question of the truth of an assertion, in comparison to an extra-scientific question, such as the relevance of the research in resolving problems of human welfare.[3] Thus, the first task for social science researchers in their search for truth is to separate "purely scientific value problems of truth, relevance, simplicity and so forth, from extra-scientific problems" (1976, p. 98). Researchers should then proceed to challenge existing theories for their truth or falsity through pure deductive logic.

Challenges to existing theories, i.e., attempts to refute the assumptions upon which the theories are based are, according to Popper, the most fruitful means toward advancing truth. In his formulation, one can speak of progress, a cumulative process toward truth as researchers appraise, refute, or fail to refute theories. Before proceeding, three of Popper's main challenges to the received methodology of logical positivism[4] are reviewed, followed by an examination of criticisms leveled against his arguments.

First, logical positivism approaches theory building by formulating hypotheses from direct observation. Popper disputed whether such a method could be naturalistic, scientific, or objective. He regarded hypothesis formulation as originating in conjecture, hunch, or even a myth. A researcher's selection of experiences or observations upon which hypotheses are formulated is personal judgement, affected by personal or historical experience. For Popper, observation could never be value free; in his own words, "all observation is theory impregnated" (Katouzian, 1980, p. 72).

Second, logical positivism's rule of demarcation for a theoretical statement to qualify as scientific was if, and only if, it was verifiable. Popper's challenge is that only those statements that can survive tests of falsifiabilty, not verifiability, are meaningful and contain scientific knowledge.

Popper's third departure from the received view concerns the growth of knowledge. Previously, researchers rejected as meaningless noises all statements that were not verified. But Popper contends all unfalsifiable statements (whether metaphysical or normative) can be meaningful, because they can evolve into scientific theories. For Popper, the growth of scientific knowledge is a cumulative process. Although hypotheses are statements initially based on conjectures, when they are tested against observation and experience for falsification, they can bring us closer to knowing the world as it really is.

Critique of Popper's Research

Although Popper recognizes that facts do not stand independent of theories, the formation of hypotheses (how researchers decide which problems to study, i.e., the origins of scientific study) is delegated by Popper to empirical psychology. The origins of research are less relevant to Popper than his concern for the "logical analysis of scientific knowledge" (i.e., methodology) (Popper, 1959, p. 31–32). Thus, Popper separates research theorizing from the process (or practice) of researching.[5]

Popper claims that knowledge is advanced by using "crucial experiments": continuous attempts to falsify existing hypotheses which are then replaced with new hypotheses that resist falsification. The flaw in Popper's claim is that no individual scientific hypothesis is ever conclusively falsifiable. Blaug (1980) points out that we always test a particular hypothesis in conjunction with auxiliary statements (i.e., assumptions). Hence, we can never be sure that we have confirmed or refuted the hypothesis itself. Popper himself has stated, "In point of fact no conclusive disproof of a theory can ever be produced; for it is always possible to say the experimental results are not reliable" (Popper, 1965, p. 50). Popper then sets out to prescribe methodological limits on the strategems that may be adopted by scientists to safeguard their theories against refutation. Thus Popper's falsification methodology degenerates, because he does not really advance on the verification methodology of logical positivism (the point of his suggesting falsification).

Blaug's critique of Popper's *The Logic of Scientific Discovery* asserts it is not a logic of discovery but a logic of justification, because the problem of how one discovers fruitful scientific hypotheses has been ruled out by Popper from the very beginning as a psychological puzzle (Blaug, 1980 p. 20). Blaug suggests that Popper's methodology is plainly normative, prescribing sound practice in sciences. In contrast to Popper, the research by Thomas Kuhn is an inquiry into the research process: a description of social factors that contribute to current and future research inquiries, i.e., the social origins of theories. The inclination to preserve theories and to render them immune from criticism is a central issue in Kuhn's description of scientific behavior.

The Process of Growth in Knowledge: Kuhn

Kuhn's challenge to Popper was a devastating critique at the heart of Popper's theory of knowledge production. Kuhn rejected the notion of knowledge as a cumulative process through which we get closer to truth. Knowledge accumulation, as a social process, is best described by a dichotomization of scientific activity into (1) normal science and (2) extraordinary, or revolutionary science.

Normal scientific activity is the routine, puzzle-solving activity of researchers. It is the realm of scientific activity where researchers cultivate further an already accepted and established historical achievement (paradigm),[6] or concentrate on resolving minor issues needing clarification to support these ruling or dominant paradigms. According to Kuhn, the majority of research activity is spent supporting previous research, rather than challenging accepted theories.

Extraordinary, or revolutionary activity takes place when serious anomalies between the accepted paradigm and reality (the empirical world) systematically occur (Katouzian, 1980, p. 94). When the search for explanations of reality are no longer consistent with the accepted paradigm's framework, the scientific community is in a "crisis" (Kuhn, 1970, p. 7), during which rejection of the ruling paradigm is stubbornly resisted by most scientists. Previous supporters fear a loss of scientific prestige and authority if the paradigm is refuted; resistance is also strong because scientists, trained for so long in the dominant paradigm find it difficult to think in terms of a new paradigm. It requires a gestalt switch in thinking, amounting to a new world view for the scientists. Kuhn contends that protagonists are effectively functioning in different worlds and resolution within the scientific community occurs not through scientific proof,[7] but through persuasion (Kuhn, pp. 148–150, 200).

Kuhn's message has be summarized as a "vaguely formulated but deeply held suspicion of cognitive factors like epistemological rationality" in regard to research and knowledge advancement (Blaug, 1980, p. 32). Kuhn's explanation of accumulation of knowledge emphasizes "sociological factors like authority, hierarchy, and reference groups as determinants of scientific behavior" (ibid.), refuting Popper's view of a systematic, logical, and rational process by which new theories come to be accepted.

Kuhn's critique of rationalist epistemology is significant because his framework establishes the beginning of a socio-historical dimension of the research process. As observed by Rose and Rose (1977) in their description of the interrelationship between natural science, technology, and society, current research is affected by a hierarchy of decisions concerning research funds, the highest problem being how much the state should allocate for research versus, for example, construction of a hospital. The next allocation decision is between disciplines, then within disciplines, and so on. Rose and Rose suggest that because science is currently a massively financed and closely controlled field, the structure of society can be more readily viewed as creating and affecting a discipline's choice of research (p. xvi). The authors conclude that politics, economics, and vested self-interests create a climate for scientific research that distorts the academic freedom image of scientists. In actuality, controls on scientific and technological research are neither neutral to interests nor unaffected by the outside social, institutional, and state structures (Rose and Rose, 1977, pp. 210–215; Whitley, 1974; and Zukav, 1979).

Knowledge Production:
Socio-Historical Approaches Beyond Kuhn

Theorizing in Sociology

Kuhn's conceptualization of the scientific community as operating in a consensual society is refuted by numerous theorists in sociology and related disciplines (Baritz, 1960; Berlin, 1966; Bernstein, 1976, 1983; Blackburn, 1972; Doyle and Harris, 1982; Foucault, 1972; Giddens, 1979; Gouldner, 1976; Levi-Strauss, 1977; Poulantzas, 1978; Ravetz, 1984; and Winch, 1958). We illustrate the critique with Allen's work (1975).

Allen claims there is a qualitative difference between, on one hand, perceiving reality as a social system pervaded by consensus and capable of experiencing only limited changes, and, on the other hand, perceiving it as an interrelated entity, beset with contradictions which are capable of transforming it. As Allen states, "the theoretical implications are enormous . . . [because researchers] are given 'model problems and solutions' which lead them to concentrate on superstructural issues, and to neglect structural [broad] ones" (pp. 42, 44). When researchers proceed in this manner, they see only limited problems and can only perceive of limited changes. In this manner, research can be viewed as perpetuating certain interests in society to the neglect of others.

The dominant paradigm in science is reflective of social beliefs prevailing in social reality (ideology). Allen suggests that displacement of one dominant paradigm by another is inevitable and inexorable because of a larger set of broadly based conflicts in society. Using research in sociology as an example, Allen argues that sociology has undertaken "conceptual adaptions" (mystifications) in contrast to "conceptual innovation," which is an alteration in the conceptual basis itself. For example the term *dysfunctions* has been introduced in social science research in order to account for social tensions and problems, not fundamental conflicts in the ordering of social members.[8] The introduction of dysfunctions is a conceptual adaptation, enabling functionalism to account for movement within systems without acknowledging social conflict. The phrase is a mystification because the conceptual basis of dysfunctions is pluralistic, institutionalistic, and democratic, and the theory rests on contributing toward the achievement of equilibrium within the existing social relations of production. In contrast, the research would be innovative if conflicts were looked upon as a disintegrating force, dividing classes and providing the stimulus for structural change.

Allen's research illustrates that the manner in which the world is viewed—in a broad sense—is important in research agendas and in theory building. His concern is that the definition of what is a social problem is fixed for sociologists, affecting future research and the criteria against which research is assessed. The importance of theories is that they embody ideas, values, and assumptions about social reality and provide a means of simplifying, understanding, and changing it through them (Allen, 1975, pp. 53–55). Therefore, he argues, because theories and research inquiries cannot be detached from social realities, they partake in social controversies, and can be used to support partisan interest.

Knowledge Production in Economics

Katouzian offers a perspective of economic research in his book, *Ideology and Method in Economics* (1980), claiming that a special brand of logical positivism, "Positive Economics," has served as the dominant criterion for economic research in the twentieth century. Positive economics theorizes neo-classical economic thought, with some of its adherents believing that a mere distinction between fact and value is sufficient for its methodological requirement. Katouzian observes numerous disagreements among economists as to what defines research as positive or normative, and he notes that confusion is exacerbated because "Positive Economics" is used to connote both the method and substance of economic theory. For Katouzian, the acceptance of positive economics is more plausibly viewed as a justification for "how we do things in economics" (p. 46) rather than a meaningful criterion for economic research (i.e., he suggests there are socio-psychological origins that are attributable to the use of positive economics as a criterion for assessing economic research).

In reviewing a number of fundamental economic theories— The Law of Diminishing Returns, The Theory of Marginal Utility, and Neo-Classical Consumer Theory—Katouzian illustrates that they are not consistent with the positivists' own minimal requirements. It has been illustrated[9] that they are not inherently testable, and upon negative results, they have not been rejected as the positivist criterion requires they should. Positivists support their theories by attaching measures to concepts which, according to their own standards cannot be measured, and supplement their theories with assumptions, when according to their own standards, the theory should be rejected. Thus, there is little to guide economic researchers in assessing whether their work meets the positivist criterion. But not only is the positivist criterion ill-defined, its insistence that growth of knowledge is based on non-subjectivity and free of value judgements misses the point that economics is, as is all knowledge, a socially constructed discipline (see also Amin, 1978; Bernstein, 1983; Blaug, 1980; Cornforth, 1973, 1980; Coward and Ellis, 1977; DuBoff and Herman, 1980; Gouldner, 1976, 1980; Hall, 1978; 1983; Heilbroner, 1980; Hindess and Hurst, 1977; Holloway and Picciotto, 1978; Hunt, 1980; Jessop et al., 1984; and Marx, 1977).

As was pointed out in the previous discussion on research in natural science and sociology, researchers are constrained by the scientific community's prevailing direction of research, the researcher's immediate (individualistic) professional and class affiliations, and the stage of economic development. Therefore, the claim by positivist economists that the formation of ideas from direct observation leads to entirely value-free theories, and is detached from social controversies cannot be supported. Moreover, it would appear that "it is both possible and desirable for natural and social scientists to be consciously 'honest'; ethical neutrality is meaningless, for indifference itself is a moral position" (Katouzian, p. 140). Again, research inquiry cannot be detached from society. Research creates social reality, and in this manner, inevitably advocates the interests of some social members over others.

Feminist Challenges to Science and Techniques of Knowledge

Perhaps the most significant challenge to the received methodologies of science, technology, history, sociology, anthropology, economics, literature, and knowledge production in general, has appeared in the latter part of this century from feminist theorists. Their challenge is as devastating as it is diverse, questioning the very notion of what is "scientific," asserting that all disciplines delimit knowledge, construct privileged access to ideas, reconstruct patriarchal hierarchies, and restrict access to power based on gender and race. These critiques extend to the very heart of debates regarding knowledge, truth, criteria for research, and social practice. By interrogating and questioning what we understand of the social world around us, these researchers seek to illuminate whether our commonsense ideas and beliefs have a genesis privileging a "masculine" model, preserving the interests of men and their dominance. In this regard, feminists debate and problematize that what is masculine or feminine is a social construction, defying simple categorization, being historically, culturally, and economically situated.

One criticism is leveled at the exclusion of females from the scientific community, and that this must inevitably affect the scientific project. The questions that are asked, the subject of inquiry, the methodology, and the interpretation of results are all affected by the gender of the scientist. Some researchers surmise that a greater prominence of females in scientific inquiry will change it. Others contend that the mere inclusion of women will not be a transforming act. A masculine perspective counts as truth within the community in order to preserve the power to shape reality, and to maintain the privileged position of white males in Western society. Challenges to institutions and structures that exclude females, establish dominance over nature and women, and exploit disadvantaged groups are among the interventions that would be necessary for there to be substantive upheaval in the scientific community.

The most fundamental critique of the scientific project for these researchers is that there will be alternative ways of developing meaningful knowledge about the world. The language and process of science, the goals and what counts as truth, the techniques and appeal to calculative regimes, and the theoretical basis applied to science all reflect gender biases in the production of knowledge. In contrast to the masculine desire for a manageable, rigorous, controllable, and commanding stance from which to shape knowledge, feminists envision the process of discovery and knowledge as a liberating and emancipatory project. Within this vision, domination and hierarchies are replaced with the integration of community and inclusionary attitudes; methodologies would embrace experience, case history, contextualization, and qualitative study; nature would be viewed as active and dynamic rather than passive, necessitating manipulation and control; and the variety of interests, biases, perspectives, and needs of nature and people would be acknowledged and privileged, rather than denied or dismissed in search of objectivity. Numerous alternatives and innovations among these theorists have emerged, and are currently undergoing debate, development, alteration, and enhancement. The nature of the feminist critique, which recognizes and problematizes the social constitution of knowledge, would suggest that any alternatives and perspectives would themselves be subject to challenges, scrutiny, and transformation; the current task at hand is to begin this process of interrogation and revision. (For a more complete account, see for example, Coontz and Hendersen, 1986; Coward, 1983; French, 1986; Gilligan, 1982; Haraway, 1989; Jaggar, 1983; Johnson, 1987; Lerner, 1986; Oakes and Hammond, 1991; and Stiehm, 1984).

Epistemology in Accounting

The previous sections illustrate the problematic search by researchers attempting to establish criteria for research, develop a methodology for research, and formulate an explanation of the advancement of knowledge. If we were to review accounting research, what criteria would we find? As has been previously suggested, all researchers, implicitly or explicitly, approach their inquiry with an epistemological affiliation, a set of beliefs and values which have historical and social foundations.[10]

What, then, are the major epistemological affiliations of accounting research? And what are the implications of the research that is generated? The review below summarizes the main controversies in accounting concerning criteria for assessing research.

Recent concerns about theorizing in accounting is illustrated in Arrington and Francis, 1989a, 1989b; Burchell et al., 1980; Christenson, 1983; Chua, 1986, 1988; Dopuch, 1980; Gallhofer and Haslam, 1991; Hines, 1989; Jensen and Meckling, 1986; Lowe et al., 1983; Neimark, 1990; Tinker, et al., 1982, 1988, 1991; and Watts and Zimmerman, 1978, 1979, 1990, among others.

Dopuch, Jensen and Meckling, and Watts and Zimmerman argue that accounting research has been unscientific, possessing normative characteristics and committing value judgements. They suggest that normative (i.e., prescriptive) research should be abandoned in favor of developing positive (i.e., descriptive) theories: those which do not declare value judgements, but instead describe what accounting *is*.

Christenson's critique of the above views (which he labels "The Methodology of Positive Accounting") centers on the issues we have already raised: "as a philosophy of science, positivism is no longer taken seriously" (1983, p. 13). The research by Christenson (1983), Hines (1989), Hopper et al. (1986), Laughlin (1987), Lowe et al. (1983), Neimark (1990), Okcabol (1989), and Tinker et al. (1982) illustrate that accounting researchers ignore many of the complexities surrounding issues in epistemology. Thus, misunderstanding abounds as accounting researchers disregard or confuse issues regarding epistemology, methodology, and terms such as normative, positive, empirical, value-free, and objective.

An important epistemological debate significant to our inquiry here, is whether theories may be unambiguously segregated into normative or positive, and whether "in those cases where a theory had been infected by values, the very act of recognizing the value judgement (usually called 'stating one's assumptions') somehow exorcises the theory of the troublesome element" (Tinker et al., 1982, p. 170). In accounting, as with other disciplines, some researchers search for value free theories, a misinformed search reflecting a failure to acknowledge the social constitution of accounting.

Boland (1982) challenges the notion that theory construction in accounting is a logical and technical process; accounting theories are not immutable, as they must be compatible with the constantly changing institutional and political characteristics of society. It is impossible, asserts Boland, for accountants to be uninvolved, objective, and value free; accounting theories are an active part of the interplay between organizational internal efficiency and organizational legitimation, societal and political interests, performance, adaptation, and ethical interactions.

The mutability and social conditioning of accounting is couched in cultural characteristics, such that culture and accounting theory are often inseparable. Citing the example of Native American culture and its emphasis on the present welfare of the tribe, Gambling observes the incompatibility with the Western cultural concept of present value of future income, and its related accounting practices. Thus, "accounting theories differ profoundly to the extent variables (such as values and cultures) governing the societies differ" (Gambling, 1974, pp. 172–174).

Accounting theory and practice become ways of knowing and communicating "reality" for conventional researchers; they eschew the mutually constitutive relationship between accounting and social reality—that social reality is constructed, not merely a reflective or representational act (Arrington and Francis, 1989a; Chua, 1988; Gallhofer and Haslam, 1991; Hines, 1988a, 1988b; Hopwood, 1984; Lowe and Tinker, 1975; and Tinker, 1985, 1991). Taken-for-granted assumptions, embedded in predominate modes of accounting research and practice, have shielded the reality construction of accounting from scrutiny. Yet recent research, subverting the claim of accounting as reality, pierces this shield from a number of theoretical platforms.

These critiques assert the following: economic reality cannot exist independent of our apprehension of it; reality is not represented unambiguously and faithfully in a system of signs or symbols (signs are social constructions and arbitrary); the economic realm cannot be severed from social and political regimes; by communicating reality we construct reality; and knowledge is indeterminate—i.e., it cannot be externally grounded—because it is legitimated through its own privileged discourse (Arrington and Francis, 1989a; Hines, 1988a, 1988b; Lehman and Tinker, 1987; and Tinker, 1991). Truth is not a technical artifact; we inevitably give the world meaning. These issues regarding meaning, discourse, and symbols are readdressed in Chapter IV.

Burchell et al. (1980) illustrate the non-reflectivity of accounting researchers, referring to scholars who view the accounting systems "as mirrors of the societies or organizations in which they are implicated. At the societal level, this has involved seeing accounting as essentially reflective of the organization of social relationships. Feudal societies are seen to require feudal accounting systems, capitalist societies, capitalist modes of accounting" and so on (p. 10). Burchell et al. view accounting as a social practice, an outgrowth of "institutional processes . . . shaped by the pressures which give rise to accounting innovation rather than any essence of the accounting mission" (p. 12).

Social practice embraces a range of acts in governing, disciplining, dominating, and constructing social members; accounting intervention participates in and reflects these practices. Miller and O'Leary (1987) refute conceptualizing accounting, particularly the development of cost accounting, as a functionally motivated stage in the refinement of accounting techniques, emerging neutrally and independently of wider social practices. Rather, the emergence of costing systems is viewed as an important calculative practice, part of the constellation of modern apparatuses of power emerging in the 1900s to create manageable, controllable, and governable persons. A variety of expert knowledges—in engineering, eugenics, industrial psychology, and journalism—converged to "work on" the person, "to be managed through a series of interventions into an enhanced state of life" (Miller and O'Leary, 1981, p. 261). The construction of standard costing and budgeting, and the resultant calculative techniques, expanded the potential of enmeshing persons into norms of efficiency and rational performance.

Hoskin and Macve (1986) examine the social practice of accounting for its penetration and intervention in bringing together power and knowledge relations. Stressing the powers of writing and education (in giving prominence to certain knowledge, in privileging certain forms of power), they assert that changes in writing enable changes in the level of discourse, and that changes in modes of learning produce new power-knowledge regimes. The power of these two educational technologies are a particularly apposite way of understanding the intervention of double-entry bookkeeping—at a point in history between A.D. 1250 and 1350 when a rewriting of texts occurred and when the first generation learned to learn in a historically new way—under examination for qualification. For Hoskin and Macve this re-writing is what produces new discursive possibilities. It is also simultaneously the point where new power-knowledge possibilities took shape (including the judicial form of Inquisition, double-entry bookkeeping, the writing of intentions). These shifts are the precursors of the modern obsession with calculation, and the manageable, calculable, and governable person illuminated by Miller and O'Leary (1987).

In theorizing about accounting, Neimark (1990) laments that such theorizing about accounting as calculative practice, as text, and as contingent on particular incidents, devoid of the interplay between the material world of work and power, and silent on the dynamics of capital accumulation, installs a methodology of accounting theory that is as disempowering as the received methodologies before it. Fascinations with the text or the worker that are merely descriptive, reinforces the status quo by overlooking the inseparability of text and discourse from the social conflicts and structural inequalities of the time. For Neimark, an emancipatory form of accounting theory and critique is necessary and feasible, one that theorizes the sites of struggle within monopoly and advanced capitalism, and the uneven economies, societies, and ideologies—globally. This broader materialist emphasis considers the significant arenas of social combat in the day to day experiences of work and survival through inter-and intra-class struggle, imperialism, and patriarchy. This radical project is not an exercise in apolitical deconstruction, but a project to socially engage accounting roles: that the presence of accounting—as a sign system, as a language of business, and as an arena of adjudication—is not related to nothingness, but to what accounting denies, prevents, or destroys. As a ritualized method of resolving conflict over wealth distribution, accounting must be theorized in its historical contextualization; only then can its theorists break from installing disempowering regimes.

Two views emerge from the above, each implying a different criterion for assessing accounting research. Dopuch, Jensen and Meckling, and Watts and Zimmerman, for example, seek to imbue the discipline and its research with concepts such as *value free, objective,* and *fact,* even though these concepts are illusory. The second view of accounting inquiry, articulated by Arrington and Frances, Christenson, Chua, Cooper, Hines, Hopper et al., Lowe et al., Neimark, Tinker et al., and others, envision the discipline as socially constituted, a social practice embedded in a socio-historical context. This latter view has implications for a criterion for assessing research, which is discussed below. In addition, a socio-historical approach to research, referred to as critical theory, is reviewed and its criterion for research is assessed.

Critical Theory: An Approach to Research

As an overview to critical theory, we refer to Laughlin's observation:

> Despite the variety of ideas which can legitimately be called critical theory, one theme is common to all: the need for critical analysis of present social configurations and the necessity for change and development of such configurations if society is to progress, with theoretical insights being seen totally in the context of such a practical emancipatory concern (Laughlin, 1985, p. 3).

One integral aspect of the Frankfurt School of Critical Theory is its approach to the question of praxis: concrete (political) efforts aimed at individual and social emancipation (Heydebrand and Burris, 1980). Shrivastava (1983) illustrates that various notions of praxis have been proposed by researchers. For example, praxis as practice guided by theoretical truth, is Marcuse's conceptualization (1964). Adorno's (1973) concern is to apply this notion to bring about change and concrete political action. Habermas's (1979a) conception of praxis[11] is summarized as the acquisition of communicative competence by all subjects, allowing participation in discourse that is aimed at liberation from constraints on interaction (Shrivastava, 1984, pp. 24–25).

Heydebrand's description illustrates that one of the objectives of critical theory is to situate social analysis within a historical context. He states:

> a critical theory of organizations ought to address a number of issues . . . it ought to be "critical" in the sense of revealing the historically imbedded, partial, and ideological nature of organizational theories rather than treating such theories merely as more or less adequate reproductions of immediately perceived phenomena. . . . Thus, such concepts as power, control, rules, resources, production, goals, output or effectiveness cannot be neutral technical terms describing nearly universal social relations; they are, above all, ideological terms relevant to political positions and strategies within specific historical settings and struggles (1978, p. 640).

The use of critical theory as a framework for research requires reflection of the nature of the surrounding social environment and its historical context (Bernstein, 1983; Held, 1980; Horkheimer, 1972; and Geuss, 1981). As was argued in the prior chapter, these aspects have been, for the most part, eliminated in neo-classical economic frameworks for research, a framework that has underlain much of accounting research. Nor does positivist or descriptive research—which has been elevated in accounting to research itself—reflect on the social origins of theories; positivists' raison d'etre is value freedom in research. What is proposed here, as an alternative theory of research, whether referred to as critical theory, emancipatory, radical, or dialectical, requires an examination of the socio-economic-political context of research inquiry.

Seeking absolute truth (orthodox epistemology) obscures the social interests that an epistemology advances. By downplaying research's effect on social conflicts, the orthodox epistemology perpetuates the status quo. The claim that orthodox epistemology offers a neutral position is rejected here: the practices and theories, and even descriptions of what is going on, of all disciplines are inevitably terrains of social conflict.

All researchers, implicitly and explicitly, choose sides in social conflict; all researchers assume interests to advocate, perpetuate, and support. Objectivity, as a basis for research, permits researchers to ignore the partisan interests that the research promotes. In contrast, this research proposes that one criterion for assessing research should be that it is reflective of the interests advocated by the research. This means that although there are unanswered questions about what "emancipation," "values," "class," etc., mean, researchers are better equipped to choose their value position with theories that explicate interests and conflict. This, it is argued, offers a more promising basis for doing research than using absolute standards that absolutists themselves cannot meet.

Accounting practice and scholarship is not just derivative and reflective of social reality, it also creates and constitutes this reality. In a conflict-based, critical perspective, antagonisms between opposing social constituencies occupy the foreground of the analysis, focusing on the evolution of relations of cooperation and conflict in reproducing collective existence. Significantly, a conflict-based approach admits the possibility that social conflict is not a conflict between equals, but involves struggles between structurally advantaged and disadvantaged groups.

Two routes were proposed earlier as a means of understanding the roles of accounting. The first was an examination of epistemological controversies that resulted in a rejection of objectivity as a socially neutral basis for conducting research. The proposal here is that one criterion for assessing research should be that it explicate the social interests advocated by the research. The second complementary route to exploring accounting's participation in society was an inquiry into the socio-historical nature of the discipline, a reflection on the socio-economic-political environment in which accounting and its literature are situated. We turn to this next.

Notes

1. Popper's framework formed a school of thought commonly called Popperian Logical Positivism, but Popper rejected this as his school of thought. We will describe his rebuke of a number of the tenets of logical positivism shortly in Kuhn's work and others.

2. Numerous researchers have documented social science researchers' desires to emulate natural science. Bernstein (1976) describes the 1950s dominant mood in the social science as a positivist temper recognizing only two models for legitimate knowledge: the empirical or natural sciences, and the formal disciplines such as logic and mathematics (p. 5). Bernstein suggests that a basic unanimity among mainstream social scientists has been the importance of developing testable explanatory theories. Not only do these researchers agree that there is a real possibility of social sciences maturing in this manner and emulating natural science, but they agree this is the direction in which the social disciplines ought to progress (p. 24). Winch (1958) claims that the idea of a social science modeled on the natural sciences involves insurmountable conceptual confusions and fallacies. See also Neimark, 1983; Blaug, 1980; Feyerabend, 1968; Tinker et al., 1982; and Zukav, 1979.

3. A more comprehensive explanation of these differences may be found in Popper, 1976, p. 901.

4. The terms *positivist, logical positivist, empiricist, descriptive,* and *objective* have been used interchangeably, resulting in confusion and controversy. In addition, their comparison to terms such as *normative* and *subjective* have further complicated their usage. A discussion of some of these issues is addressed in this research; for additional discussion see Bernstein, 1976; Christenson, 1983; Lowe et al., 1983; and Tinker et al., 1982.

5. This contrasts with Kuhn's approach (and his concern for the context of discovery) and Habermas's concern of practice, which is also reviewed.

6. Kuhn's use of the word *paradigm* is confusing. In his first usage it referred to a "disciplinary matrix": the "entire constellation of beliefs, values, techniques and so on shared by members of a given community"; a paradigm is also described as one of the components in the matrix (Kuhn, 1970, pp. 175, 182). Researchers have identified a variety of meanings given to the word in Kuhn's research (Masterman, 1979).

7. Previous researchers (and to some extent this includes Popper) have idealized the scientific community's agreement on epistemological issues in their discipline, which dismisses the current crisis the scientific community is having concerning the socio-historical dimensions of the natural sciences (see Zukav, 1979).

8. Allen cites the work of Coser, Freidman, Silverman, Dahrendorf, and Millson as examples.

9. See Katouzian, 1980, pp. 55–71; Christenson, 1983; Lowe et al., 1983; Neimark, 1983; and Tinker et al., 1982.

10. See, for example, Burrell and Morgan, 1979; Cornforth, 1980; Eagleton, 1976; Feyerabend, 1970; Giddens, 1979; Gouldner, 1976; Marcuse, 1964; Pirsig, 1974; Seliger, 1979; Shaw, 1975; Therborn, 1980; and Tinker et al., 1982.

11. Habermas' research is extensive in a number of research programs in addition to critical theory. Also his research has been the subject of numerous reviews and critiques. See, for example, Habermas, 1970, 1973, 1975, 1979a, 1979b; Bernstein, 1976; Doyal and Harris, 1982; Held, 1980; McCarthy, 1978; and Thompson, 1983.

CHAPTER *IV*

SOCIAL CONFLICT, THE STATE, AND THE ROLE OF ACCOUNTING LITERATURE

In contemporary accounting research there is little consensus on "the" role of accounting, rather, there are numerous views regarding the purposes and outcomes of accounting, each warranting further explanations of accounting's participation in society. Some researchers emphasize the socially beneficent nature of accounting because it provides information to financial statement users, thus assisting in the efficient allocation of resources. Others propose that accounting is partisan, benefiting only certain groups by emphasizing the role of efficiency, neglecting issues of equity, and adopting an unreflective view of the social implications of accounting research.

The previous chapter indicated that in order to understand and assess accounting's role, an analysis of the broader socio-economic-political environment is required. Such a research program already exists in the literature: one that contends accounting theories and pronouncements are "excuses" and "rationalizations" (Watts and Zimmerman, 1978, 1979; Jensen and Meckling, 1980; and Benston, 1982a, 1982b). However, the suggestion that accounting theories are used to obscure political disagreements begs further questions about the social origins that guide accounting theorizing and research, the functions of those social practices, and the institutional mechanisms by which they are discharged.

One mechanism, the profession's literature—a form of communication and social discourse[1]—is a reflection of accounting's role. What is provided below is a rationale as to why accounting literature as a mode of symbolic exchange or social discourse is a fruitful area for gaining access to its role. Briefly, the research focuses on a view of accounting and its literature as social beliefs and instruments in social conflicts. Only by understanding how accounting practices (research, theories, activities, literature) are produced, i.e., the social context that originates them, is it possible to show who they serve and begin to reconstruct them to serve different purposes.

Before proceeding with the journal analysis, it is necessary to establish the social origins of accounting practices (auditing, consulting, researching, and so on), to provide the setting in which these activities emerge. Therefore the following section examines the nature of society in which these practices emerge—once again our study necessitates a socio-historical understanding of the surrounding environment.

The Structures of Societies

In order to understand the exact character, direction, and momentum of social practices such as accounting, (i.e., in order to understand why and how such activities are as they are), they need to be related to the social circumstances that give rise to them. These circumstances include two fundamental aspects of any society: how it organizes to produce the means of existence for its members, and how that social product is distributed. Both aspects are integral to understanding accounting practices as we know them today, and as they could be in the future.

The importance of production and distribution activities is underscored by Cornforth (1980):

> considering the ways we relate ourselves to one another in social life, it becomes evident . . . that the social mode of production of the material means of life, the ways people relate to one another in keeping reproduction going and in appropriating its product . . . have been of primary importance as the man-made conditioning circumstance of all social life (p. 264).

Cornforth emphasizes that the relations between people as producers in economic reproduction is crucial in constituting society and social change; different production relations provide a basis for defining different types of societies, such as primitive, slave, feudal, capitalist, socialist, communist. Different types of societies are described and differentiated both as systems of material reproduction for their social members and in terms of the conflicts these social systems imply. The description that follows begins with simple primitive societies, and progresses toward more complex industrial societies.[2]

Primitive Societies

In primitive communities, the means of subsistence (food, clothing, and shelter) were produced entirely within the tribe. Members formed hunting bands, made weapons and tools (technology), cooperated through a division of labor (cooperative organization), and distributed the prey within the collective (rules of distribution) (Habermas, 1979, p. 134). As long as these communities barely produced enough to keep their members alive, (maintaining only a subsistence level of existence) all members were held to similar economic levels, little social differentiation was possible, and there was no exclusive or private access to the means of production. Females and males may have had a fluid or organized division of labor, but a hierarchy of importance, power, or domination among these divisions was likely non-existent.[3]

A number of events occurred which raised productivity above the subsistence level, thereby providing communities with a surplus; members were then able to negotiate about its distribution. A surplus, or surplus product, has been defined in one context as that which is beyond what is necessary to satisfy the indispensable physical needs of the immediate producer (Cohen, 1978). Cohen distinguishes this from other important but different concepts of surplus. For example, surplus has been conceptualized as production beyond what is necessary to satisfy the historically developed needs of the producer. Another concept defines surplus as production appropriated by the exploiting non-producers.[4]

Pure Commodity Societies

Early communities generally developed various customs and ceremonies to prevent any excessive wealth accumulation by individuals (Mandel, 1975). Permanent agricultural surpluses permit a social division of labor, i.e., vocational specialization to take place, such as craft activities. Within this form of social reproduction, independent primary (immediate) producers exchange the products of their specialized activities for the necessities of life, a relationship referred to as "pure commodity production" or "simple commodity circulation" as compared to more advanced forms of commodity production such as contemporary capitalist society (see Blanke et al., 1978, and Hirsch, 1978).

Pure commodity production assumes that each producer owns his or her tools of production and that there is no separation of the ownership of labor from that of capital. Competition between the primary producers (who alone exchange what they have produced in simple commodity circulation) ensures that equal values in terms of labor will be exchanged. When product exchange is based on labor equivalences, forces are at work which help maintain a social integration and an economic equilibrium, and prevent the emergence of privileged and less privileged groups, as there is little private accumulation of capital.

Other Social Orders: Slavery and Feudalism

Equal exchange ideal-type society (characterized by ownership of the means of production) may be contrasted with social orders in which unequal exchanges take place. Societies where the ownership of the means of production (e.g., land) was controlled by masters (private landowners who were not the primary producers) appeared in ancient Greece, Rome, and other Mediterranean societies—a slavery mode of production (Cornforth, 1980).

In medieval Europe, feudalism was based on large private estates allotted to individual producers (serfs) bound by various relations to the feudal lord (Habermas, 1979). A central form of feudal society was characterized by the serf working a portion of the time for the feudal lord without any compensation, as a condition for the serf to maintain his or her position on the estate, i.e., an appropriation of surplus labor referred to as "labor rent" (see Cohen, 1978).

How is the exchange of labor for products, and the division of the social surplus conducted in slave and feudal societies? The following example, provided by Mandel (1975) explores this question. On seventeenth-century plantations in Portuguese Africa and the West Indies, slaves worked for six days on the plantation; only on Sundays were they allowed to till the plot of land from which they produced their own food. In this example, the laborers work seven days, but receive the product of only one day's work. The balance of the laborer's product (a social surplus) is appropriated by the plantation owner. This exemplifies the unequal exchange of labor for products, and a division of the social surplus whereby the landlord receives six days of the slave's labor time, for which the slave receives nothing. In this unequal production relation, the endemic social conflict was repressed by a superstructure of law, ideology, religion, social custom, and coercion (Allen, 1975; Cornforth, 1980; Habermas, 1979; Marx, 1977; and Rude, 1980).

The foregoing indicates how social orders can be characterized and distinguished from one another. Societies differ in the forms of specialization, the division of labor, the techniques used in economic activity (technology), the purpose of production, (e.g., whether production is for immediate use or is intended for exchange), and as to whether there is surplus labor, and the way it is appropriated.

Primitive societies are characterized by their lack of surplus labor because they are usually producing only at subsistence levels. Under slavery, however, surplus labor may appear as the portion of the slave's product retained by the master after providing for the slave's means of survival. Surplus labor may be appropriated in a variety of ways; in slave and feudal modes, a superior exerts authority over the producers' labor power, a relationship based on the "forcible domination of one section of society over another, assured by a combination of (threat) of violence and ideology" (Cohen, 1978, p. 83).

These comparisons, illustrating that social relationships interrelate with economic production and distributional characteristics of a social order, suggest that one method of defining and distinguishing societies is to observe the method of appropriating its surplus. It is the method used here because it is at the root of social conflict, and thus gives character to ideology, beliefs, and accounting theory.

Conflict in Capitalist Society

In an industrial, capitalist society, production and distribution are characterized by a complex set of social relationships between social members, involving private ownership of property and wage labor. One characteristic of capitalism is that production is not for use, but for exchange. Exchange under capitalism contrasts with exchange in other social orders: simple barter is a form of exchange in which each side wants a specific use value in exchange for his or her product, as might occur in primitive societies. In pure commodity production societies, maximum exchange value for products is sought, but any excess of what is needed to service and replace the producers' means of production is devoted to personal consumption, not the accumulation of capital. What distinguishes capitalism from other social systems, as economists since Adam Smith have pointed out, is that parties to an exchange aim to obtain maximum exchange value, with a view to increasing capital accumulation.

As with other social orders, there is a social surplus in contemporary capitalist societies. Surplus value (the monetary form of the surplus product) is produced by wage laborers; the owners of production extract surplus value by way of profit. It is through the socially relative convention of property rights that capital owners come to share in social production. They participate, however, on an unequal basis in that, qua capitalists, they do not make any personal sacrifice of their own life's experience, but benefit from the efforts of the labor of others. The laborers receive a wage but they produce a product that, in real terms, has a new value greater than the wage paid to produce it. The difference between the produced value and the cost of reproducing labor is surplus value and represents, in the final analysis, unpaid labor (Althusser and Balibar, 1970; Mandel, 1975; and Marx, 1977).

One final characteristic of capitalist societies is the condition that induces the immediate producer to work, and thereby produce surplus value. The dependency of the immediate producer (laborers) on the owner of the means of production is secured economically through the labor market, legally through the institution of the labor contract (Habermas, 1979) and, as with other societies, through various social, political, and ideological structures. Unlike the property-owning capitalist, the only means of subsistence for the worker is the sale of his or her own labor.

Thus contemporary society, like other societies, is characterized by conflicts due to unequal exchanges between parties (e.g., immediate producers and financers). Conflicts of interest continue throughout the productive and distributive spheres, "not just at the end of the day when the fruits of their (labor's) productive activity are distributed amongst the different factors of production" (Hill, 1981 p. 259). The tensions are seen as a permanent, pervasive factor, in all areas of social life, conditioning all aspects of social behavior (Allen, 1975; Campen and Mac Ewan, 1982; Dale et al., 1976; Heilbroner, 1980; and Poulantzas and Miliband, 1972).

Having only partially established the origins of these tensions, a number of important questions remain that are relevant to the role of accounting and its literature. One aspect, addressed in the next section, is the interrelationship between social conflict and economic disturbances and resolutions. Habermas (1979) suggests that these disturbances, referred to as crises, have their origins in the economic systems of capitalism, but symptoms of the crises are displaced into strains within the cultural and social order. The research here seeks to examine how these crises are managed, and to explore how accounting (theory, practice, and literature) participates in these socio-economic changes.

Developments of Economic Strains and Impediments

Economic crises are distinctive features of capitalist societies, and they originate in the conflicts and contradictions of that social system. These types of conflicts—manifested in periodic crises—lend a special character to the kinds of social practices (accounting, ideological, political, etc.) that a society assumes. By examining periodic crises, e.g., long waves, we can examine one specific origin of accounting practice.

Long Wave Theories

MIT researchers argue that while business cycles of three to seven years have received the attention in management and political literature, long-term economic change has received little attention (Forrester, 1978 and Mitchell, 1965). The fifty-year repeating rise and fall of economic activity, called the *long wave* or Kondratieff cycle, is identified as a period including a decade of depression, thirty years of technical innovation and active capital investments, and finally ten years of economic uncertainty while the growth forces of the past subside. Numerous researchers agree that these long periods of expansion and contraction can be observed empirically; they disagree, however, as to the mechanisms behind the evolution of long waves.

Forrester offers one explanation of how the economic long wave is generated:

> The process involves an overbuilding of the capital sectors in which they grow beyond the capital output rate needed for long-term equilibrium. In the process, capital plant throughout the economy is overbuilt beyond the level justified by the marginal productivity of capital. Finally, the overexpansion is ended by the hiatus of a great depression during which excess capital plant is physically worn out and financially depreciated on the account books until the stage has been cleared for a new era of rebuilding (1978, p. 6).

Researchers contend that this process applies regardless of technological change; innovation and technology have little impact on the long wave process. In identifying these economic crises and their generation, the above theory does not examine social relationships underlying the phenomenon. Yet these relationships are crucial to understanding how production and distribution evolves, develops, or is halted by crisis.

Socio-Historical Views of Economic Crises

Wright (1975) supports the general theory that periodic economic crises emerge from the contradictions inherent in the process of capital accumulation. He notes, however, that because there is little consensus on which contradictions are most central to understanding crises or even how the contradictions in accumulation should be conceptualized, these theories have been unable to provide an adequate understanding of economic crises. Wright contends that these theories are not incompatible, as long as they are viewed as part of a historical process. His theories may be used to illustrate the dialectical nature of economic crises.

Wright argues that at different stages of capitalist development the accumulation process faces different dominant constraints and impediments. These impediments are not exogenous factors; rather, they are generated within the accumulation process itself. In order for the capitalist production to continue, these constraints must be overcome; the solution to a dominant impediment at a given stage generates new impediments which constrain the accumulation process in subsequent stages. It is in this sense that the impediments to accumulation are contradictions; they are contradictions because the solutions in one period eventually become impediments to accumulation in future periods. Thus, economic crises can be understood as a transition era, from one configuration of constraints on accumulation, to a new set of emergent constraints (see Wright, 1975, pp. 5–6).

These arguments provide Wright with the framework to integrate a number of competing theories used to explain periodic economic crises (e.g., the problem of realizing surplus value, a falling rate of profit, or the contradictory role of the state, ibid., pp. 12–30). The view of economic crisis as endemic in capitalist society underlies analysis by a number of researchers (see, for example, Amin, 1978; Davis, 1980; Heilbroner, 1982; Post, 1982; and Wolfe, 1981). What distinguishes Wright's analysis from those of the MIT school is that Wright's view of capital is that it is a social relationship, rather than a physical object or resource (Wright, 1975, p. 6) (See also Ollman, 1976).

Mandel's analysis (1975) may be seen in a similar vein, as an explanation of economic crisis within the internal dynamic of the accumulation process itself, emphasizing the inherent tendency of accumulation to undermine the foundation of its own success (see Rowthorn, 1976). Mandel's analysis of long waves relates:

> the diverse combination of factors that may influence the rate of profit (such as a radical fall in the cost of raw materials, a sudden expansion of the world market or of new fields of investment for capital, a rapid increase or decline in the rate of surplus value, wars, and revolutions) to the inner logic of the process of long-term accumulation and valorization of capital, based upon the spurts of radical renewal or reproduction of fundamental productive technology. It explains these movements by the inner logic of the process of accumulation and self-expansion of capital itself (p. 145).

The contradictions in capitalist social systems affect and reflect a variety of social conflicts, and have the potential to affect economic crises. For example, although a reserve labor army (unemployment) holds down wage rates (costs of production), a lack of wage income impedes the business objective of realization of profits because of a lack of markets (consumers) for the goods produced. The welfare state illustrates another contradiction in that the state's support of the needy, for example, through Social Security, is initially beneficial to firms that might otherwise have to incur these costs directly (for example, through pensions). However, as the state becomes increasingly obligated to make these payments, the state competes with business for funds and drives up the cost of capital and taxation to business.

The study of capitalist society viewed in terms of contradictions, impediments, and economic crises is an approach emphasizing the dialectical process of a wide variety of technological, economic, and socio-political-ideological factors. More important, the dialectical nature emphasizes the pervasiveness of tensions, social conflicts, and impediments and contradictions from which specific forms of accounting theories, literature, research, and activities originate. We reject a dogmatic economic interpretation of these crises, and give weight as well to the primacy of language and signification through literature practices.

The preceding illustrated a number of the reasons for the periodic problems of securing profits. The twentieth century has illustrated, with periodic slumps, booms, depressions, and recessions, numerous examples of unresolved solutions to the problems of industrial development. The economic problems are dynamically interacting with social relationships during all these periods. Some tensions are resolved, and new ones emerge. What are the means for resolving these tensions? How are they managed in contemporary society? We turn to these issues next.

The Roles of the State and Accounting

In order to explain accounting research and literature, it is necessary to examine the context within which these activities originate. The prior sections have discussed a number of aspects concerning this environment. Among them are: the linkage between production requirements and social relationships, and an economic environment of crises and tensions. The contention in this book is that in any society there are elements which reproduce the essence of that social order, i.e., shape and maintain the social structure of that society.

Contemporary society is characterized by social relationships based on unequal exchanges and, as in other social orders, this creates a potential for ongoing conflicts and tensions. Periodic economic crises are manifestations of these unresolved tensions, partly as a result of the inequalities built into the social and economic structure. We observe, however, that production does take place, even within this environment of pervasive tensions, and thus our interests focus on how social tensions are displaced, managed, or regulated so that production endures. In most societies, there are social relationships and institutions (the educational system, the legal system, etc.), that provide for the society's reproduction; social order is achieved by socializing, policing, educating, and so on.

The state is considered by many researchers as a primary means of dispersing and managing social conflict. The state is not merely a background factor in society, nor a passive element. It takes an active role in managing social tensions, and it achieves this role, in part, through accounting practices. This aspect of the state gives it particular significance for our research: the statutory and regulatory relationship between the accounting profession and the state. In its most basic terms, the relationship is one of both dependency and autonomy, because although the profession receives its status from the Securities and Exchange Commission and congressional approval, it maintains a self-regulatory dimension at the same time.

Consensus and Pluralistic Theories of the State

One view of the state and the political process asserts "Political parties are basic institutions for the translation of mass preferences into public policy" (Key, 1967). This view of the state as neutral and committed to common interests is often combined with a recognition of some conflicts of interest in society—a view or theory usually defined as pluralism. Dahl's view is that communities search for ways of adjusting conflicts, e.g., through the state, so that cooperation and community life will be possible and tolerable (1972, p. 5). Pluralism assumes a diversity of interests, objectives, and power both between and within groups, organizations, and societies. Diversities are essential in pluralistic theorizing. By assuming many sources of power and control, no group can obtain ubiquitous control or domination. Pluralism is a particular expression of equilibrium analysis, representing conflicts as aberrations from equilibrium, but the possibility of achieving equilibrium is always present (Allen, 1975).

Many researchers, characterizing the political process in terms of pluralist theory, assert that the state organizes the numerous interests of its society in a benign manner. Pluralism assumes the state has the ability to act in this fashion and that it is a voluntarily or exogenously determined agency, not influenced by its own internal structure (for example, the interests of its own members). The political system is conceived of as a mutual benefit organization—a problem-solving mechanism for the good of all (Lindblom, 1982, p. 12).

In summary, pluralist theory views the state as a problem solver, and although tensions exist in society, conflicts are merely temporary. Equilibrium and consensus are the dominant long-term characteristics of contemporary society.

Recent failures of the state to manage social antagonisms has led some theorists to place the blame on excessive claims of competing interests, and the absence of economic growth and prosperity needed to meet these claims. This reformulation of pluralism has been referred to as the overloaded government thesis: a wide range of social groups imposing too many demands on the responsive apparatus of the liberal democratic state (Crouch, 1979; Lowi, 1979).

Is the environment of contemporary society one of underlying consensus, and is the state thus a mere conduit for achieving mutually beneficial goals? The failure of the state to provide for the common interest provides some researchers with evidence that it does not really serve that purpose. Lindblom (1982), a past president of the American Political Science Association, criticizes theories of the state as a mutual benefit organization because they fail to explain "the frequency with which government subsidies turn out to be for the benefit of the well-off rather than for the disadvantaged" (p. 15). George and Wilding (1976) question the impartial arbitrator view, which does not explain why privileged groups grant concessions to non-dominant groups, but prevail on the larger issues.

The view of the state as a public benefit institution and neutral in the interests it serves has been rejected from various theoretical positions. A capture theory of state regulation, where the regulators are seen as being captured by the interests it is supposed to regulate, was promoted by Kolko, who observed in his study of regulation for the period 1900–1916, "Federal economic regulation was generally designed by the regulated interest to meet its own end, and not those of the public or commonweal" (Kolko, 1963, p. 59). Research by Weinstein (1968) also concludes that in the early 1900s the implementation of state regulations was based on corporate demands. Regulations and laws were viewed as necessary for survival because it could alleviate public criticism by providing a (sometimes false) assurance that corporations would be held accountable for their actions. Merino and Neimark (1982) provide an account of the role of regulations in maintaining the credibility of financial markets.

Stigler (1971) also rejects the notion that state regulation is based on the public's interests. Stigler's research is associated with "the economic theory of regulation" (Posner, 1974, p. 343) which imposes an economic rationality to previous capture theories of state regulation. Briefly, Stigler suggests that the mechanics of the political apparatus are such that the state can be viewed in terms of supply and demand. Thus, state regulation is a product acquired by those who value it most and are willing to pay the price. Those who are willing to pay the highest price receive the benefits of the state, (e.g., favorable legislation regarding entry by new rivals, subsidies, and other distributions of state resources).

Stigler's theory is differentiated from previous capture theory by Posner (1974) who insists Stigler's theory is "more precise" and "committed to the strong assumptions of economic theory generally, notably that people seek to advance their self-interest and do so rationally" (p. 343). Stigler's early capture hypothesis did admit the possibility that the state might be ruled by powerful economic interests rather than by democratic processes. This disconcerting implication was quickly laid to rest by Peltzman's (1976) addendum to Stigler's theory. However, neither formulation resolves how or why certain interests can capture state favors, and at other times cannot (Davis, 1980, 1981; Edwards, 1979; McCraw, 1975; Okcabol, 1989; Okcabol and Tinker, 1990; Pollard, 1968; Wolfe, 1981). Nor do they explain how the state may be responsive to the interests of capital in general, as well as the sometimes conflicting interests of specific capitals (e.g., financial versus industrial, indigenous versus international, and competing capitals within an industry sector).

Conflict-Based Theories of the State

The alliances and policies adopted by the state may be viewed as reproducing capitalist social relations of appropriation. It is argued that this is a core function of the state: its role in reproducing society.

Post's research of the Civil War points to the state's interest in supporting broad objectives of industrial capital. He contends that a solution to constraints on industrial expansion of capital was achieved by the political effects of the Civil War, "a consolidation of the hegemony of industrial capital at the state level" (1982, p. 48). The obstacles to expansion in the 1840s and 1850s included an inadequate supply of labor and the lack of markets necessary for the realization of profits because of the self-sufficiency of plantations. The state provided resolutions to these obstacles and an impetus to expanding the reproduction of capital by liberalizing immigration laws, enacting the Homestead Act of 1862 (granting land to those who would farm it), and the abolition of slavery (ibid.).

State concessions and constraints, perpetuating the social relation of property ownership, are reflected in legal institutions which address the interests of advantaged groups whose overall interests are advocated (Tigar and Levy, 1977). These conclusions differ from Stigler's capture theory of specific interests, in that Tigar and Levy's broader view of the state and society proposes that "legal forms foster particular social relationships in economic life" such that individuals are subordinated to the interests of advantaged groups—a relationship of power enforced by laws.

These views imply that the state in contemporary capitalist societies acts as an instrument of a dominant class, a view sometimes called the instrumentalist view. This theory claims that the state acts in the interests of capital because a dominant class holding economic power, sometimes considered "elitist," (see Miliband, 1969) is a class that can pressure the state to be receptive to its interests. The result is that the capitalist class does not govern, but rules (Miliband, pp. 66–67; see also Baran and Sweezy, 1966; Crouch, 1979; Hill, 1981; Holloway and Picciotto, 1978; and Wright, 1978).

Poulantzas rejects this view of the state as a "tool of manipulation or instrument of the ruling class" (1978). Poulantzas establishes that capital comprises factions whose interests may often be in conflict. It is thus necessary that the state not be an instrument of one class, but it maintain a relative autonomy. This enables the state to determine the appropriate actions it should pursue in the overall interests of capital, providing a balance when the interests of specific factions conflict.

A number of critiques have been leveled against a dogmatic interpretation of Poulantzas's theory of the state (sometimes referred to as structuralism). One problem is an assumption that the state acts for general, not specific factions, and that the latter do not obtain state actions in their favor. However, such is not always the case, as exemplified by the financial sector in Britain which has obtained control of state policy to the possible detriment of the long-term interests of capital as a whole (Crouch, 1979, pp. 26–27; Jessop, 1980, 1982)

An even greater problem with a structuralist approach is its inability to explain the state's responsiveness to working class demands, and the insistence that the state is only concerned with benefiting the dominant class. First, this ignores the extent to which the dominant class mistrusts the state and tries to limit its activities, "hence the extravagant measures they take to leave no area of the polity uncovered by their own organized activities" (Crouch, 1979, p. 53). Second, there is a crucial flaw in the theory's negative rationality concerning any state action in favor of the working class. Structuralism is a form of economic class reductionism in that no matter what the state does, structuralism interprets the action as beneficial to the dominant class. In other words, state policies in favor of the working class are interpreted as concessions that are necessary to support the capital class's interests. This ignores the point, however, that as much as capital might benefit from offering concessions, it would gain more if they did not have to be made (Crouch, 1979; Mosley, 1982; Panitch, 1981).

Indeed, working class interests are represented in the state's policies, and the very suggestion that the state is relatively autonomous must imply that, within the polity, there is support for labor. Labor's interests must be present in the state, otherwise relative or limited autonomy is a meaningless notion. In other words, if labor was not represented and was neither a concern nor a threat, the state could be totally tied to capital interests, no concessions would be necessary, and relative autonomy and legitimation would not be needed.

Gramsci (1971) contributes to our understanding of the state's role in terms of relative or limited autonomy. He views the state as an alliance of class factions, recognizing that the interests of a ruling class are achieved in real social settings by means of alliances. For Gramsci, the social democratic state secures the conditions necessary for the reproduction of capital—not by force or coercion—but by organizing a consensus among these alliances, in regard to political, moral, economic, and cultural objectives. When the state obtains legitimation, secured by broad and popular consent, Gramsci speaks of hegemonic domination; the consensus-based leadership obscures social conflicts, commands loyalty, and establishes domination through consent. The state retains its relative autonomy because of the need to win the consent of alliance members, and earns that consent by mediating conflict from an ostensibly impartial position. In this limited sense, the state's autonomy is real and cannot be reduced to a class deterministic view of the state with the corollary that capital owners may suffer real setbacks in the short term for their long-term interests.

Thus, problems with the instrumentalist and structuralist approach have led researchers to re-theorize, rejecting the view of the state as responsive only to certain dominant class interests. Instead, these interests are served by state support for general factional interests.

In departing from a class reductionist approach, some researchers argue that the state supports the general interests of capital because it is dependent on the capital accumulation process for its own existence (e.g., Lindblom, 1977; O'Connor, 1975; and Offe, 1984). For example, the state relies upon taxation for its own existence, and thus, for the state to maintain itself, it supports that mode of production which is likely to continue to sustain its existence. Lindblom (1977) suggests that in the relationship between the state and business, the latter receives a privileged position because jobs, economic security, etc., rest in the hands of business. If the state were to ignore business interests, the consequences of economic distress could potentially bring down a government (as exhibited numerous times in the twentieth century alone). Thus, the state has an alliance with business not only because this alliance serves business, but because it is also in the interest of the state itself.

State involvement with business, however, creates a realm of additional tensions and contradictions in the reproduction of the society. The state's interaction covers a wide range of activities, and whether these are in the form of regulation on corporate activity, or transfer payments such as Social Security, they are sources of interference in the free enterprise system. Regulation can be a source of constraint on capitalists seeking economic growth; similarly, the state's involvement can be a source of competition in borrowing. Therefore, although the state's actions are directed at supporting the capitalist mode of production, these actions and the coalitions that the state enters into to reproduce society become sources of tensions and impediments to the reproductive process (e.g. the fiscal crises of the state, O'Connor, 1975).

The state's involvement in capitalist reproduction also creates what Habermas (1969, 1975, 1979) describes as a "legitimation crisis"; as state intervention becomes institutionalized and expected, it also becomes expected that the state can achieve more and more. O'Connor (1975) also refers to increased pressures upon the state because of increased expectations, which creates for the state an ideological, as well as economic, legitimation crisis.

The nature of these tensions (the state's legitimation problem and interference in financial markets) are such that they penetrate broad spheres of social life. This requires the state to "constantly reorganize an historical complex of general economic and political and social relationships" (Holloway and Picciotto, 1978, pp. 28–29), supporting a view of the state as concerned with the reproduction of society through the management of economic, ideological, and numerous other spheres of society (Barone, 1982; Cohen, 1981; Gamble and Walton, 1976).

George and Wilding (1976) also illustrate the complexities of the state's management of tensions, and the contradictions that evolve, because, as in all societies, a particular set of beliefs and values is required to regenerate that society. They suggest a social democratic society that relies on an ethic of self-help, freedom, individualism, competition, and achievement. The (ideological) problem in contemporary society, which is intensified with state involvement, is the strain on these notions. In the case of individualism, for instance, a constantly moving compromise develops between values of security and humanitarianism on the one hand, and self-reliance in the competitive order on the other (pp. 106–117).

One last example illustrates the complexities, interrelationships, and changes in managing societal tensions. The twentieth century may be viewed, not in terms of "harmony and consensus" for the British government, but a situation represented by "well-managed crisis avoidance." Middlemass argues that between 1916 and 1926 the British political system established, with great difficulty, a new form of harmony, which lasted until the mid-Sixties "when the much vaunted 'consensus' was seriously, if not fatally, disrupted" (Puxty, 1984, p. 18). Middlemass demonstrates that "even before the era of full suffrage they [British governments] had discovered how to exercise the arts of public management, extending the state's powers to assess, educate, bargain with, appease or constrain the demands of the electorate, raising to a sort of parity with the state the various competing interests and institutions to which voters owed allegiance" (ibid.).

Hall (1983a, 1983b, 1983c) also claims that the 1960s marked a breakdown in the state's ability to manage through consensus (Gramsci's hegemony of consent) and ushered in a different regime for managing conflict: one that is coercive and authoritarian. These descriptions of the social democratic state illustrate its role in management of social tension directly, as well as indirectly through laws, education, politics, and other ideological mechanisms, what Gramsci (1971) refers to as the armor of consent.

The management of tensions, and the conformity between social, political, and economic life that is required by the state in reproducing the society, embraces a range of activities including the promotion of certain beliefs. This is frequently accomplished by working through the society's cultural apparatus to obtain ideological conformity and cohesion. Rather than concentrate on economistic preoccupations of the state, the preceding discussion illustrates the importance of the state's role in ideology. In the next section we discuss ideology, and particularly the ideological apparatus of the state, in terms of its role in the reproduction of society and its management of social tensions.

Managing Conflict and Ideology

Two aspects of ideology, and their implications concerning accounting's role in society, are focused on here.[5] The first concerns the relationship between ideology and epistemology (the latter was the subject of Chapter III); the second addresses the role of ideology in managing social conflict. Under both aspects, ideology reveals itself as a quasi-autonomous component in the reproduction of society, thus demonstrating its importance apart from economic origins.

Ideology versus Real Knowledge

The epistemological discussion in Chapter III illustrated numerous attempts to establish definitions of truth and fact (see Blaug, 1980; Kuhn, 1970; and Popper, 1965). Researchers sought to establish methodological criteria for the social sciences, that, like the natural sciences, would be objective, ignoring the controversy that the natural sciences had not achieved this rule of demarcation (Bernstein, 1976 and Zukav, 1979). The objectivity versus subjectivity dichotomy frequently juxtaposed ideology as antithetical to objectivity. Ideology was described in terms of beliefs and attitudes, and could not contribute to real scientific knowledge.

Conceptualizing ideology as an idea, or an illusion or "false consciousness," implies that ideology must be expunged from research in the quest for truth. Such a view of ideology ignores the socio-historical aspects of the research process (see Kuhn, 1970) that ideology cannot be expunged from research or life because, as viewed by Althusser, it is the "social cement"; "it is only through ideology that conscious subjects live" (Giddens, 1979, pp. 179–181). In contrast to previous views of ideology as mere false beliefs or false consciousness, to Althusser, ideology is functionally necessary in every society. It is the medium by which individuals relate to the world in a socially signifying way because it interprets and mediates what individuals experience (Althusser, 1971; Laclau, 1977).

In this regard, ideology is not passive, it is a social practice, an indispensable source of social cohesion enmeshed on its own in the reproduction of society (autonomous from any economic deterministic conceptualization). Ideological practices shape expectations and possibilities, and as socially constructed practices they are incorporated into language, culture, and tradition (Arrington and Francis, 1989a, 1989b; Coward and Ellis, 1977; Derrida, 1976; Knights and Willmott, 1985; Ryan, 1982; Sassoon, 1978; Weedon et al., 1980; Willis, 1980; and Woollacott, 1982). As the symbolic means by which we conceive, formulate, interpret, and act on the world, ideology has a significant effect in mediating the allocation of resources, rights, and obligations in society (Althusser, 1971, 1976; Derrida, 1976, 1978; Gallhofer and Haslam, 1991; Gramsci, 1971; Hall et al., 1978; Hirst, 1976; Lehman, 1990; Pateman, 1988; and Tinker et al., 1988).

In addition, the concept of ideology as a socially signifying practice implies that its meaning and cohesion are particular expressions of the society in which that ideology exists. Forms of ideology are determined within the social whole, and as an element of social formations, ideologies relate to that society. The next section focuses on one characteristic of contemporary society of particular concern to our study: how conflicts in society are managed, and the role of ideology in that regard.

Ideology and Social Conflict

The social role of the state and the accounting profession in managing conflict through ideology—as adjudicators and arbitrators—is integral in regenerating contemporary society. Ideology may mystify and distort reality in various ways. One important form is the universalization of sectional interests. In this mode, ideology claims that sectional interests represent the interests of the community as a whole. By generalizing sectional into collective interests, this form of ideology promotes sectional interests without disclosing that effect.

Giddens (1979) suggests that a second attribute of ideology is that it denies contradictions that would otherwise translate into social tensions. In this manner, ideology may displace conflict by obscuring, disguising, or denying the real locus of conflicts.

A third form of ideology involves a naturalization of the present by portraying the existing state of affairs as natural. This form of ideology sustains the status quo by presenting current social relations as fixed, immutable, or natural (i.e., reification). By viewing the existing society as natural, potentials for change or movement from the status quo are inhibited. The naturalization attribute is illustrated by Barthes's claim that myth is an ideology because it depoliticizes and dehistoricizes phenomena (Barthes, 1972; Chambers, 1974).

These forms illustrate how ideology may condition social practice, affect social change, and ameliorate conflicts and tensions. In the prior sections the state was viewed as a contested terrain, in which different constituencies seek to advance their interests through state mechanisms. It is the ideological form of social management that this study focuses on. Rather than examining the state's use of coercion and force, the emphasis here is on cohesion through ideology.

Accounting forms part of the state's ideological apparatus, not in a property sense, but as a powerful instrument available to the state for managing social tensions. Thus, an objective of the empirical research is to assess how the accounting profession participates in creating and reflecting society, i.e., how does the profession contribute toward giving the world meaning? In order to examine how the profession presents the world, the research reviews accounting and business literature for their ideological expressions.

A Semiotic Analysis of Accounting Literature

This study is a content analysis of ideological themes (discourses) appearing in accounting and business literature (the *Journal of Accountancy, Accounting Review,* and *Fortune* magazine) for the period 1960 though 1973. The selection of journals, and the choice of time period is explained afterward. Below is a description of semiotic analysis, deconstruction, content analysis, and their relationship to this study.

The development of content analysis, as a research methodology, was prompted by the "need for systematic and objective determination of various types of communication significance" (Gerbner et al., 1969, p. xi). Content analysis was developed as a method of exploring meaning from various forms of communication in which data are classified according to a unit of analysis (such as a word), thus providing a quantitative expression of the message.

In the past, studies of literature and other forms of communication have used informal review techniques, as well as content analysis (codings) in an attempt to evaluate opinions, norms, cultures, political disputes, etc. As an example of an informal appraisal, Sutton et al. published an analysis of the views and opinions of business executives in their book *The American Business Creed* (1956). The purpose of the study was to determine, by reviewing managerial publications, what message of society managers promoted (and what issues were not discussed and were therefore omitted from the agenda). The central concepts of the business publications were classified according to themes, but not quantified, as is often done in content analysis. In contrast, McClelland's study, *The Achieving Society* (1961), sought to determine the interrelationship between culture, achievement, and industrial development through a content analysis of children's literature (see also Chenoweth, 1974; Kerlinger, 1973; and Neimark, 1983).

An ambitious content analysis was undertaken by Galambos (1975) who attempted to capture the public's perception of big business and the changes in perceptions over the three generations of his study, 1890–1940. Galambos decided that his goal— to seek a better understanding of the past—could best be achieved by examining middle class occupational literature during the period. He chose to study commonsense subsets of the middle class (e.g., farmers, organized laborers) and to determine their attitudes by coding their occupational journals.

Under the usual assumptions of content analysis, the coding scheme is purposely developed in order to provide a conformity to the information being studied. For example, Berelson (1954) states, "Content analysis is a research technique for the objective, systematic and quantitative description of the content of communication" (Berelson, 1954, p. 489). Content analysis has traditionally viewed messages as being sent with a specific meaning, message, or intention, and thus, the objective was to code these consistent expressions.

This type of approach has been criticized on a number of grounds. For example, it does not explain the subject's initiation into communicative forms, thus treating the subject as merely a bearer of structural properties, without explaining how the subject (and therefore the subject's practices) are constituted. Previous approaches regarded the actor's definition of the communication as definitive, rather than making the speaker's enunciative practices the effect to be explained (Edgely, 1979; Ellis, 1980; Habermas, 1979; Heck, 1980; and Keidel, 1981).

Because past approaches ignore the social constitution of communication, there is no explanation of the relationship between ideology, language, and society. In contrast, current research in semiotics and deconstruction attempts to explain the relationship between different societies, cultures, social practices, and the communication produced. This view of communication admits ideology into the analysis as a component in its ultimate symbolization and interpretation, important in its formation of life (practices) and what Gramsci calls "common sense" (see Hall, 1980a, 1980b, 1982; Lacan, 1977; and Bird, 1982).

In this research, the approach to literature analysis regards discourse as socially constituted, recognizing that the subject's subconscious is formed by pre-signified cultural themes and premises, i.e., a prior socialization. The prior socialization brackets and sustains what is considered natural, meaningful, and immutable (Barthes, 1972; Coward and Ellis, 1977; and Saussure, 1960). Discourse as a social practice, an interaction of language and ideology by which the world is meant to mean, suggests a distinctively different approach to communication than traditional content analysis. In this manner, semiotics, deconstruction of the text, and epistemology are interrelated and linked, because they are ways of presenting the world and giving meaning to the world. Epistemology concerns how we are meant to know through our thought processes, of which discourse is a part. Discourse analysis (or semiotics), views discourse as information exchange and a mode of communication which is culturally modified, recognizing that social behavior, norms, and conflicts are embodied in communication.

Symbolic forms are not mere reflections of "real" phenomena; they enjoy an independent status of relative autonomy in that no absolute truth or final meaning can be attributed to signs. The importance of autonomous symbol systems is under-lined by work in semiotics, a literature treating the symbolic (and thus the ideological) realm as pre-signified. This relative autonomy is illustrated by observing that language symbols—signs—are arbitrary in that the meaning associated with the same words can change with the speaker, the receiver, the situ-ation, and previous articulations, creating a history of expres-sion (Coward and Ellis, 1977). By stressing the arbitrary nature of the sign, Saussure illustrates that the sign is independent of any specific material object, and there is no natural connection between the signifier (sound) and the signified (concept). The principle of the arbitrariness of signs underscores the ambigu-ous relationship between a sign and its referent, and most im-portant, because of this arbitrariness, rejects a privileged status to the referent and a derivative status to the sign or sign system (the latter includes languages, pictorial representations, ac-counting financial representations, etc.)

The autonomy of all systems or representation (writing, music, graphic representation) elevates meaning production systems to a new status: they are independent terrains of con-flict whose outcomes cannot be resolved reductively by referring to an economic base or some other primary realm (Blumer and Gurevitch, 1982; Curren et al., 1982; and Ryan, 1982). Derrida extended Saussure's arguments by showing that not only do signs and their referents have an independent status, but differ-ent modes of signification (writing, speech, music, etc.) also pos-sess relative autonomy to one another (Saussure, 1960 and Derrida, 1976, 1978).

Derrida's contribution to deconstruction of the text emerged out of a rejection of modernism, in which social science searched for truth, as a historical movement and growth toward one truth for which one method would evoke this state of enlightenment. In contrast to modernism, postmodernist thought, and decon-struction in particular, embraces self-reflection and a critical search for that which is denied, repressed, excluded, privileged, and reified in the text. By opposing the closure on knowledge of modernism and its appeal to possessing a superior claim on truth, deconstruction seeks to identify voices excluded from the narrative.

To reflect on the text means to challenge what is silenced, to reject the privileged text as having any legitimate claim of superior knowledge, and to search for that which is repressed and denied. Feminist theorists and writers on race illustrate that by pervasive exclusion of females, people of color, and the poor from (his)story and narrative they are excluded from power; rewriting and re-inserting their narrative challenges this repression, demonstrates the contested terrain of our knowledge of the past and present, and establishes a prominence and a powerful voice to those denied access to these terrains of conflict (Bell, 1987; Gilligan, 1982; Hirsch, 1989; Johnson, 1987; Joseph and Lewis, 1981; Lehman, 1992; Lerner, 1986; Pateman, 1988; and Stiehm, 1984).

In revealing its instability, Derrida's play on the text dichotomizes, defers, and brackets words to unveil the lack of author[ity] in linguistic practices. Similarly, accounting symbols do not merely reflect the world but re-present it in structuring the meanings and common sense notions through which individuals engage social reality. Linguistic and ideological symbols, such as financial reports that bracket and categorize (asset/liability, revenue/expense, profit/loss), are activities not independent of economic and other terrains of social struggle; they are prior to them in that they dictate the terms of access to these realities.

The symbolic realm merits privileged attention for another reason: it has assumed major prominence because, increasingly, the capitalist state has assembled an ideological apparatus for producing the social cohesion needed for capital accumulation. Accounting's discursive practices are vital components of this ideological apparatus, symbols that are loosely tied to their referents and can be "made to mean" in ways that serve different social interests.

The examination of accounting and business literature in this research is aimed at assessing the journals' participation in discursive practices and how the journals shape consciousness by subtly associating, connotating, bracketing, and putting closure on what is considered meaningful. Thus the study to follow illustrates the role of accounting literature as an ideology in creating and reflecting meaning in the world, and thus its participation in social conflict and appropriative practices.

Notes

1. Examples of the different conceptualizations of literature and discourse may be found in the following sources: Bird, 1982; Coward and Ellis, 1977; Eagleton, 1976; Galambos, 1975; Hall, 1982; Horkheimer and Adorno, 1972; Lacan, 1977; McClelland, 1961; and Sutton et al., 1956.

2. The social structures referred to as primitive, pure commodity production, slavery, feudalism, and capitalism have received considerable attention in literature concerned with historically portraying the developments of society (historical materialism literature). They have been chosen here to illustrate certain tendencies of social relationships. See Habermas (1979), however, for a critique of dogmatic versions of social evolution using these social structures.

3. Researchers suggest in early life, from 3.5 million years ago to 800 B.C., early gatherers and hunters most likely lived in flexible, egalitarian groups. Evidence of flexible work arrangements and behavior variability refutes the inevitability of a sexual division of labor. However, there is overall consensus that currently all human societies have some sort of division of labor along sex lines. Although women have participated in all spheres of social life—farming, fishing, shopkeeping, trading, ruling, medicine, religion, and rebellion—throughout history, the record also reveals differences between females and males in status, roles, wages, and expectations. See Ciancanelli, 1980; Coontz and Henderson, 1986; French, 1986; Jagger, 1983; Kessler-Harris, 1981; Lehman, 1992; Lerner, 1986; Pateman, 1988; and Stiehm, 1984.

4. Hill (1981) defines surplus product as that portion of economic activity which is left after covering the purchase of raw materials, replacement of tools, machinery, and buildings worn out in the course of production and providing labor with the means of subsistence (see also Mandel, 1975 and Wright, 1976).

5. There are numerous controversies surrounding the topic of ideology, some of which are discussed in this research. See also Allen, 1975; Blackburn, 1972; Burrell and Morgan, 1979; Eagleton, 1976; Feyerabend, 1970; Giddens, 1979; Gouldner, 1976; Lodge, 1975; Marcuse, 1964; Pirsig, 1974; Plamenatz, 1976; Potter, 1973; Ravetz, 1984; Seliger, 1979; Shaw, 1975; Therborn, 1980; and Winch, 1958.

CHAPTER V

THE DISCURSIVE REALM OF BUSINESS AND ACCOUNTING

The journal review of business and accounting literature, assessing an array of discourses appearing in the *Journal of Accountancy*, *Accounting Review*, and *Fortune* magazine between 1960 through 1973, analyzes over 1100 articles. Before presenting the results, the following sections describe the criteria used in selecting journals, the details of the semiotic classification (content analysis), and the choice of a time period. The last section provides a guide to the presentation of the results.

The Choice of the Journals

Fortune magazine, much quoted, widely circulated, and dedicated to covering business and related topics, was chosen to represent the popular business press. Economic issues, domestic and international conflicts, government regulation of business, politics, and forecasts, are among the regular features, as well as coverage of specific industries and companies.

The popularity of *Fortune* is reconfirmed by the publication *Magazines for Libraries* (Katz and Katz, 1982, 1977), which describes *Fortune* as:

> probably the best-known business magazine in America. . . .
> The purpose remains much the same, to give objective reports
> on business and industry so that readers may make decisions
> concerning investments. Students and teachers take a broader
> view and often turn to it as an indicator of current American

thinking about business in general and certain business situations in particular (1982, p. 192).

In this way, the magazine can be said to constitute and shape, as well as re-present, popular business ideology, providing a popularized discourse on the world of business.[1]

Accounting Journals

Two accounting journals were selected, intending to capture a diversity and range of accounting discourses. The *Journal of Accountancy*, chosen for its "practical" orientation, and the *Accounting Review*, known for its "theoretical" perspective have, over the years, significantly widened their difference in publication perspectives. The *Accounting Review*, sponsored by the American Accounting Association, began publication in 1926 with the objective of being an independent journal fostering academic research. As an alternative to practitioner-oriented publications, the *Accounting Review* was intended to provide a forum for scholarly research (Previts and Merino, 1979, pp. 216–217), and has been assessed as a "core research journal" in *Magazines for Libraries* (Katz and Katz, 1982. p. 411).

The *Accounting Review*'s prominence and command over academic research has been documented in a number of accounting literature reviews. Williams observes:

> The *Accounting Review* (AR) has the potential to influence the development of ideas in accounting research. The basis for this assertion is the frequently replicated results that, for at least the last fifteen years, accounting academics have perceived *AR*, along with the *Journal of Accounting Research* (JAR), to be an important indicator of accounting research acceptability (1985 p. 300, referencing Coe and Weinstock, 1968 and 1983; Benjamin and Brenner, 1974; and Weber and Stevenson, 1981).

In contrast, the *Journal of Accountancy*, first published in 1905, is oriented as a popular-practice publication, currently enjoying the "largest readership of a magazine of this type," (1981 circulation 220,000, *Magazine for Libraries*, 1982, p. 413). Considered to be the "official organ" (ibid.) of the American Institute of Certified Public Accountants (the Journal's publisher), its practical and professional stance is in marked contrast to the more esoteric, theoretical, and statistical articles appearing in the *Accounting Review*, which are authored mainly by academics. The *Journal of Accountancy* publishes articles written primarily by practicing CPAs, individuals in business, and accounting and government administrators, as well as academics. Alternatives to using the above accounting journals were limited because many accounting publications available today began publishing after the period of study.

General Information on Classifying the Journal Texts

The analysis of literature in this research stands in contradistinction to traditional content analysis, which by assuming that communication is objective, ignores its social constitution. As indicated previously, the approach to discourse that is adopted here views discourse as a social practice and socially imbued, reflecting subtleties taken for granted as well as the predisposition and prior socialization of the subject.

Acknowledging the mass media's potential in shaping consciousness, this research aims to capture the journals' creation and reflection of the social world, assessing their participation in discursive practice. Through their subtle associations, and by putting closure on what is considered natural, meaningful, or commonsense, social life is defined. Viewing these discourses as an ideological practice, we observe how the media conceals domination, denies rights, and is part of wealth appropriation (Gramsci, 1971; Hall et al., 1978).

In order to capture these meanings, journal articles were reviewed and classified into a discourse category. The discourse category is the basic unit of analysis for this study; it is the classification category for which each of the articles are coded. All articles are coded into one or more of these discourse categories. The discourse category is an ideological theme aimed at affecting a redistribution of income between social groups; the categories are active, participatory, and as a socially signifying practice they are the commonsense threads that give the world meaning (Althusser, 1971; Giddens, 1979; Gouldner, 1982a, 1982b).

As a preliminary introduction to these discourse categories, Table I lists the twenty-five *Fortune* discourse categories and Table II presents the eighteen accounting discourse categories that emerged. Note, however, that the subtleties of the discourse categories may not be apparent from this summary list. The attributes of each discourse category will be described and illustrated in detail in presenting the results of the empirical study.

Table I
Discourse Categories and Configurations:
Fortune 1960–1973

Discourse
Category

Configuration A: *Support and praise for the state's benevolent role in promoting harmony and consensus.*

#1   Advocating and praising government's assistance to business;

#2   The importance of the state's responsibilities to its citizens;

#3   The state's role as a neutral arbiter in balancing interests and contributing to social harmony.

Configuration B: *Criticism of state interference and philanthropy.*

#4   The state's interference hinders growth and development; deregulation is advocated;

#5   Welfare state policies are critiqued as impediments to growth and oppressive to all members of society.

Configuration C: *A consensual view of society and business, emphasizing shared, community objectives.*

#6   Managers and the wealthy benefiting society as industrial statespersons and philanthropists;

#7   Praise for managerial insights, creativity, and leadership in organizations;

#8   Pursuit of profit is universally beneficial;

#9   Praising domestic growth for its benefits to all social members;

#10   People's capitalism: widespread ownership ensures managers are responsive to society.

Configuration D: *An appreciation of the individualistic, competitive nature of society and the business community, and the will to survive.*

#11   Social Darwinism; in society and business, as in nature, survival of the fittest;

#12   Encouraging individualism;

#13   Promotion of material wealth as a measure of success;

#14   Management planning and authority is essential;

#15   Monopolies, oligopolies are improvements in competition;

#16   Economic rationality justifies corporate concern for social improvements;

#17   Labor strikes are subject to the harsh realities of the market.

Configuration E: *Championing American interests, values, and business practices in international affairs.*

#18   It is natural for the United States to compete internationally for markets and further capital accumulation;

#19   The U.S.'s international role as a powerful protector is vital to ensuring freedom and preventing communist threat;

#20   Market capitalism is a benevolent force throughout the world.

Configuration F: *Science and Technology.*

#21   Omnipotence of science, technology;

#22   Omnipotence of computers in particular

***Fortune* Configuration G:** *Sundry categories.*   #23, #24, #25

Table II
Discourse Categories and Configurations:
Accounting Literature
Journal of Accountancy and *Accounting Review*

**Discourse
Category**

Accounting Configuration H: *Critique of state intervention and promotion of self-regulation.*

#26   Self-Regulation is superior to state intervention;

#27   Support for the authoritative institutions and mechanisms of the profession;

#28   Accounting is responsive to financial statement users;

#29   Professionalism ensures limited regulation is universally beneficial.

Accounting Configuration J: *Accounting benefits business and society by assisting in the efficient allocation of resources and economic growth.*

#30   Assisting business is a benevolent responsibility of the accounting profession;

#31   The efficient allocation of resources is a common objective for society in which accounting plays a crucial role;

#32   Domestic growth is universally beneficial; accounting contributes toward this goal.

Accounting Configuration K: *The profession is devoted to protecting the public interest; this is a natural role, ensured by the independence of the profession, and enhanced by accountants' ethical nature and personal commitment.*

#33   The profession celebrates its ethical practices;

#34   Accountants have a natural ability to serve as public statespersons;

#35   Accountant's independence ensures third party protection;

#36   Protecting the interests of accountants also protects society.

Accounting Configuration L: *Advocating the use of statistical techniques, and the expertise of accountants in developing computerized information systems.*

#37   Statistical techniques are advanced for a range of applications in auditing and accounting research;

#38   Praise for accountants' expertise and natural role in developing computerized information systems.

Accounting Configuration M: *Promoting the international benefits of accounting; praising its contribution to economic and social freedom, international trade and competition, and global democracy.*

#39   Advancing international freedom and democracy;

#40   Praising United States competition in international markets, and accounting's contribution to U.S. success;

#41   Accounting's contribution to the global benefits of market capitalism and growth.

Accounting Configuration N: *Sundry discourses.*

#42, #43

The tables indicate that the discourse categories have been grouped according to configurations, wherever possible. Configurations are groupings and aggregates that capture the similar connotations, and overlapping subtleties of interrelated discourse categories. The advantages of presenting configurations is that they convey the unique messages of the discourse categories as well as their interrelated messages. Therefore, the configurations, similar to the discourse categories, are ways that the world is made to make sense. Table III provides a summary of the number of articles, issues, and the percentage of the issues reviewed for the three journals reviewed in the study. In the case of the *Accounting Review* and *Fortune*, for every issue in the sample, all main and feature articles were coded: 223 articles of the *Accounting Review* and 701 articles of *Fortune* magazine (i.e., the only articles excluded were those of special departments).

Table III
The Number of Articles and Issues Examined and the Percentage of All Issues Reviewed for
Fortune, *Journal of Accountancy*, and *Accounting Review*

Journal	Number of Articles Examined	Number of Issues Examined	Percentage of Issues Reviewed*
Fortune	701	84	50%
Journal of Accountancy	218	137	82%
Accounting Review	223	14	25%

* Note: The percentage is based on the following:
         Fortune, published monthly;
         Journal of Accountancy, published monthly;
         Accounting Review, published quarterly.

The coding of the *Journal of Accountancy* was limited to its editorials; 218 were reviewed. Editorials offer another view of how the world is presented, another form of communicative act, and another form of social practice using language. The editorials offer an opportunity to study a form of discourse which, by its own nature, directs itself explicitly at forming opinions, directing attitudes, and interpreting and creating the world. The editorials claim that their purpose is to emphasize what is important.[2] Editorials explicitly state the attribute of all articles and editorials—they shape and create commonsense notions and social beliefs and by their dialectical nature, contribute to conflict.

The final outcome of classifying and coding the discourse categories is referred to as a percentage, or score. The percentage is the figure presented in the tables as the summary statistic of the empirical results. All editorials and articles are treated equally throughout the classification; the goal was to obtain a percentage that could provide comparability between the publications. For each year the percentage represents the frequency of each discourse category in the journal for that year. Thus the percentage may be interpreted as the portion of all feature articles or editorials devoted to a particular discourse category in a given year.

A Periodization Analysis

The objective of this research is to study accounting's participation in social conflict in capitalist society through an analysis of its discursive practices. One feature of capitalist society—ongoing conflicts over the distribution of wealth—is never fully resolved. It is inevitable that periodic crises of severe economic and social antagonisms must be endured. During these periods numerous changes in society take place: new economic resolutions are formed, new managerial styles are adopted by the state, political coalitions dismantle and new ones form, and so on. Crisis periods, ushering in new communicative strategies and new discursive patterns, reinforce new alliances by shifting the ideological terrain. An examination of accounting literature reveals its participation in ideological struggles, its changing presentation of the world, and its changing patterns of discourses.

With this in mind, the criterion for the selection of a time period was that there be shifting economic and social patterns, a period of crises in which the state apparatus (and thus accounting) would be subject to a changing role, and a changing style of managing conflict. The period selected, 1960 through 1973, offers these properties and is supported from three different perspectives presented below. Each view illustrates changing patterns in society over the fourteen years, and each of the three analyses points to two distinct sub-periods within the 1960–1973 era. This difference between the early Sixties and the early Seventies will be used in the empirical analysis to trace accounting's discourse during these years—collectively and in terms of sub-periods.

The first perspective is a materialist review, concentrating on economic conditions, such as profit rates and unemployment. The postwar years prior to 1966 are described under this perspective as a general period of prosperity in which there was an increase in both the pre-tax and post-tax rate of profit (inflation adjusted). In addition, the period was characterized by a growth in real wages, increasing at approximately 2.1 percent per year from 1948 through 1966, while the unemployment rate during these years was approximately 4 percent.

Because of these and other economic characteristics, the 1950s to the early 1960s have been referred to as the postwar boom, which changed to stagnation and then stagflation (stagnation with rising prices) during the late 1960s. Real pre-tax profit and after-tax profit peaked in 1966 and then started falling. In real terms, the stock market index also stagnates around the same time (actually a bit earlier, as befitting its function of trying to anticipate the future). Between 1960 and 1980 the index falls sharply—51 percent in real terms. Growth of real wages slows sharply after 1965 and they start to fall after 1972. In addition, the unemployment rate increases sharply between 1966 and 1973.

The economic conditions that prevailed from the late 1960s into the 1980s display all the symptoms of an economic crisis, including a buildup of excess capacity, a slowdown in productivity, and crucially, a falling rate of profit, (Mandel, 1975; Shaikh, 1983). Shaikh argues that, ". . . both the boom and slump were regulated by the movements of profitability" (Shaikh, 1983, p. 15), and from the late 1960s onward, this has imposed real limits on the efficacy by intervention of the Keynesian model.

The second perspective is an account of socio-political-ideological developments during these years, reflected in discursive practices. For Hall et al., (1978; Hall, 1983a, 1983b), the earlier period of this study is a time in which the foundations of postwar consensus were consolidated. In the United States, consensus was epitomized by President Lyndon Johnson's Great

Society and the welfare state, the adaptation of capitalism and of the labor movement to the mixed economy solution, and the commitment to the free enterprise side of the Cold War. Hence this period was characterized by wage controls (and price guidelines), social contracts, national economic plans, and continuous consultation between representatives of the leading protagonists in society. The result was an attempt to confine the labor movement within the framework of capitalist stabilization: "to finding a solution to the class struggle within the framework of a mixed economy in which private capital set the pace" (Hall et al., 1978, p. 228). It was the inability of this hegemonic consensus to deliver the goods that precipitated its collapse in the late 1960s, and ushered in a new authoritarianism, the "hegemony of coercion" (Hall et al., 1978; Hall, 1983a, 1983b). From the socio-political-ideological perspective, one sub-period, the early and mid-Sixties, was a period in which social cohesion was achieved through consensus, followed in the next sub-period, the late Sixties and early Seventies, by a social cohesion informed by coercion.

Fortune's own subject's-eye view is the third perspective. *Fortune*'s description of the period of 1954–1973 appears in an article entitled "The 500: A Report on Two Decades" (*Fortune*, May 1975) which divides the period into several mini-eras. The first era (1954 through 1957) began with a "rather exhilarating discovery—that the United States was in an era when economic growth, and rising profits would be the norm." The second period was less agreeable, a severe recession began in the second half of 1957 through 1958, and another recession in 1960–1961. In the third period, 1962–1965, *Fortune* reports that the business news was consistently good. There were no recessions, no inflation to speak of, and real gross national product bounded up vigorously every year. Profit margins expanded steadily, reaching a record 6.7 percent in 1965.

Fortune describes the next era, 1966 through 1970, as having a distinctly different environment for the Fortune 500. The report in 1966 was growth accompanied by turmoil, and high prosperity was considered ephemeral. The new situation was inflation, and "all the dislocations that went with it." Commentaries during this period emphasize high interest rates, strikes, inventory adjustments, controls on capital movements overseas, and pressure on the dollar. In 1970, the United States suffered its first recession in almost a decade, and profit margins of the Fortune 500 fell to 4.7 percent. But there was an excitement, Fortune notes, in the era of the late Sixties, due to the growth of conglomerates and the merger boom.[3]

The next and last period, 1971 through 1973, witnessed a slowdown of merger activity. Inflation soared to record levels, and the dislocations now included wage and price controls. There were sales gains, but to a great extent they were ficti- tious, the product of inflation rather than higher real volume, and profit margins sank to dismal lows, a shade below 4.7 per- cent on average for 1971.

In summary, the three analyses above, a materialist-eco- nomic perspective, a socio-political-ideological analysis, and *Fortune*'s own overview, support characterizing the years 1960 through 1973 as a period harboring crises. Each view justifies a claim that two sub-periods, approximately 1960–1966 and 1967–1973, differ in terms of their economic characteristics and social, political, and ideological perspectives.

These views also have implications for the periodization framework that is used to analyze the data. In using a 1966 break point to separate the fourteen years, the two sub-periods are 1960–1966 and 1967–1973. However, a rigid interpretation of this division would be most unfortunate as it ignores the lags and feedbacks that constitute economic crises and the accompa- nying changes in political structures, social relationships, and discourse. Therefore, a range of break points were considered in order to capture lagged or staggered effects due to the transi- tions in the period; break points of 1966, 1967, 1968, and 1969 were used to analyze the data. As the results were generally robust and comparable across these periodizations, we present the results in terms of the two divisions: 1960–1966 and 1967– 1973.[4] Because of the voluminous nature of the data, aggrega- tions were made wherever possible in presenting the data.

Discursive Activity of Fortune

The presentation of the results begins with *Fortune*. Table IV summarizes the average percentages (for the fourteen-year period) for the seven Configurations, A through G, for *Fortune*.

Table IV
Discursive Activity of *Fortune*
1960-1973

	Discourse Category #	Average Percent
Configuration A: Support and praise for the state's benevolent role in promoting harmony and consensus.	1	3.5
	2	1.7
	3	<u>3.1</u>
		8.3%
Configuration B: Criticism of state interference and philanthropy.	4	9.1
	5	<u>3.7</u>
		12.8%
Configuration C: A consensual view of society and business, emphasizing shared, community objectives.	6	2.9
	7	4.5
	8	4.9
	9	4.6
	10	<u>0.7</u>
		17.6%
Configuration D: An appreciation of the individual-istic, competitive nature of society and the business community, and the will to survive.	11	12.3
	12	5.7
	13	6.0
	14	2.1
	15	2.0
	16	2.0
	17	<u>0.9</u>
		31.0%
Configuration E: Championing American interests, values, and business practices in international affairs.	18	6.6
	19	3.5
	20	<u>2.9</u>
		13.0%
Configuration F: Science and technology.	21	11.6
	22	<u>1.4</u>
		13.0%
Configuration G: Sundry categories.	23, 24, 25	<u>5.0%</u>
Total (Greater than 100% due to rounding)		100.7%

Fortune Configuration A

Configuration A is an aggregate of texts supporting the state's involvement in achieving social consensus. Articles in Configuration A describe the state as a positive instrument of change and encourage its participation in a wide range of activities. The articles insist that the state should be held responsible for assisting business and protecting the economic and social well-being of its citizens. In Configuration A the state is portrayed as

---

Table V
Fortune **Configuration A:**
Support and praise for the state's benevolent role
in promoting harmony and consensus.

Percentages Devoted to Configuration A:

1960–1966	8.4%
1967–1973	8.1%
Decrease	0.3%

Discourses in this configuration include:
♦ Advocating and praising government's assistance to business;
♦ The importance of the state's responsibilities to its citizens;
♦ The state's role as a neutral arbiter in balancing interests and contributing to social harmony.

---

an arena where different interests are represented, preserved, and protected in a manner accomplished by mediation and consensus, not coercion. Advocating the state's involvement in a broad range of affairs makes sense, it is argued, because the state represents the community and national interests. Configuration A advances social cohesion and a unity of society by portraying the state as a benevolent mediator and protector of its members' interests; for this reason Configuration A is referred to as a consensus view of the state.

Referring to the results in Table V, the quantity 8.4 percent indicates that during the seven-year period of 1960–1966, 8.4 percent of Fortune's texts conveyed a consensus view of the state (the 8.4 percent being an average for the seven years). Similarly, 8.1 percent for 1967–1973 means that a consensus view of the state was expressed, on average, in 8.1 percent of the *Fortune* articles coded during the seven-year period of 1967 through 1973 (351 articles). The 0.3 percent decrease over the period reflects that there was little variance regarding the consensus view of the state during the years of the study.

Why is the consensus view of the state so consistently promoted in *Fortune* magazine during these fourteen years? How do the discourses mediate the social conflicts characterizing this period? And how does Configuration A contribute, along with other discourses during this period, to forming a representation of the world that makes sense? To answer these questions, the discourse categories that comprise Configuration A are described in more detail below.

Discourse Category # 1, "Advocating and praising government's assistance to business," includes texts describing the state as an important ally of business interests, and thus, of society's interests. Articles of this genre stress what is beneficial for business is also good for the whole economy. The state's assistance to business is described not as a transfer of resources from some segments to others but as an act of efficiency and benevolence for the community at large. Therefore, articles in Discourse Category #1 universalize business interests into the interests of the community as a whole. For example, one article's call for a tax cut suggests it will benefit all social members because it will free the economy and promote growth incentives (*Fortune*, January 1963, p. 67).

Taxes are viewed in Discourse Category #1 as distorting market freedom, implying that freedom and a satisfactory distribution of wealth is to be found in the extant marketplace. A decrease in taxes, in order to stimulate growth, is considered the proper role for the government's taxation policy, emphasizing the need to assist business. Promoting growth, development, and expansion, is expressed in terms of its collective benefits and as a national priority because it benefits the entire community. However, supporting growth as automatically beneficial overlooks potentially harmful consequences of growth (externalities) imposed on others. (Some industrial growth, for example, has resulted in harm to the environment, and in involuntary changes in communities and the uprooting of families.)

Articles in Discourse Category #1 advocate subsidies and assistance for specific industries (promoting the interests of specific capital), or call upon the state to resolve disputes among segments of business (intra-capital disputes). In addition, the state is called upon to preserve the interests of capital in general over specific capitals. For example, one article accuses government of inaction in cutting the production of uranium, and contends that this is at the root of an oversupply and inefficiency in the marketplace. (*Fortune*, February 1964, p. 108.) Other illustrations include a call to the SEC to regulate conglomerate disclosure in order to encourage real, not illusionary, growth through takeovers. The article is not promoting the elimination of takeovers, but that government could help discourage some corporations from merely piling up assets rather than generating growth.

In summary, Discourse Category #1 includes articles that propose that the state be a partner in promoting business interests by stimulating economic growth and managing the economy, responsibilities that are natural roles for the state to assume. Any conflicts that arise between business interests and others, it is argued, should be resolved by the state with an emphasis on economic reality. In general terms, this category is reserved for articles envisaging a positive involvement by the state in assisting business, rather than an apprehension about state intervention and interference.

Discourse Category #2, "The importance of the state's responsibilities to its citizens," contains articles that emphasize the state's responsibility for protecting all of its constituencies. The articles discuss issues such as shelters in case of atomic attack, the need for defense programs, the beautification of the country and the resolution of civil rights issues in terms of the state's responsibility. The state is described as a protector and an actively involved planner, and contrasts with articles condemning state involvement as improper interference.

Discourse Category #2 represents the state as an able resolver of conflicts that originate from conflicts over the distribution of wealth. The articles never discuss the fundamental issues underlying these tensions, but merely blames the state for failure to manage conflicts between businesses, employees, minorities, and other nations. Defense issues are presented in terms of the state's natural role as protector of its citizens, in contrast to counter-discourses which relate defense to issues of imperialism, exploitation, or a means of realization of profit. The latter discourses are excluded from the text of *Fortune*.

In Discourse Category #3, "The state's role as a neutral arbiter in balancing interests and contributing to social harmony," the state is portrayed as independent, egalitarian and fair, and as an arbiter in conflicts between special interests. A belief in the state's independence is essential to its productivity as an organizer of consensus. For example, one article describes the need for the state to set basic national objectives and to promote shared values. The state is called upon to recognize and solve "increasingly bitter conflicts of narrow special interests . . . and yet provide direction for all" (*Fortune*, September 1971, p. 88). Thus, the image of society conveyed by these *Fortune* discourses is one in which there is a respect for the interests of all individuals and groups, and that all interests deserve attention by the state. This type of portrayal fails to reflect on the social construction of interests, in that fundamental inequalities may be perpetuated by discourses.

We combine the three discursive categories described above, because, collectively, they describe the state's active involvement in achieving social consensus. They similarly represent the state as responsible for serving and balancing a plurality of interests. Additionally, the three discourse categories define the state as a positive instrument of change in a wide range of activities. Therefore, Configuration A encourages a view of the world in which the state mechanism can be relied upon to assist business through tax policies, to provide fallout shelters, and to protect its citizens through defense policies. Support and justification of the state's involvement in a broad range of affairs is explained in terms of national interests.

Configuration A, by advocating the role of the state as a protector of society's interests, and as a benevolent force in distributing wealth, is ideological because the configuration creates and reinforces a certain set of beliefs about the state. These beliefs include expectations that the state will assist business, and therefore, there is an expectation that business will flourish. Configuration A also advocates, as common sense, that the state will contribute to consensus between groups with different, often conflicting interests. These views reinforce an expectation that the entire community can be better off because of the state's interactions with these conflicting groups and its ability to mediate and resolve conflicts.

The early period of this study has been characterized as economic boom years, and the years of the supportive welfare state. Thus a commonsense view of the state that would coincide with the socio-economic circumstances of this period would be a consensus view with the attributes of Configuration A. During the later years of the study, however, the economy's strength deteriorates as profit rates begin to fall and rising inflation rates strain the economy. Why does Configuration A remain a consistent percentage of *Fortune*'s literature? In order to answer this question, there is the need to address any other discourses directed at the state that appear in *Fortune* during the period of study. In the following section an alternative to the consensus view of the state is discussed; this is then integrated with the results of Configuration A into a comprehensive review of state ideologies reflected in *Fortune.*

Fortune Configuration B

Discourse Categories #4 and #5, combined in forming Configuration B, cover an array of articles presenting generally negative views of the state, views that are quite distinct from the consensus view of the state advocated in Configuration A. Articles in Configuration B emphasize the state's intervention in the marketplace as an impediment to business, placing onerous regulations upon business that cause a wide range of economic inefficiencies. Additionally, the state's bureaucracy and welfare policies are blamed for creating and maintaining economic deterioration and other social ills. These negative views comprising Configuration B are referred to here as the "interference view of the state."

TABLE VI
***Fourtune* Configuration B:**
Criticism of state interference and philanthropy

Percentages Devoted to Configuration B:

1960–1966	9.5%
1967–1973	<u>15.7%</u>
Increase	6.2%

Discourses in this configuration include:

♦ The state's interference hinders growth and development, deregulation is advocated;

♦ Welfare state policies are critiqued as impediments to growth and oppressive to all members of society.

The data indicate an increasing percentage of articles are devoted to Configuration B in the later years of the study; such articles appeared 6.2 percent more frequently during the period 1967–1973. To an increasing extent, *Fortune* articles reinforce a belief that the state is to blame for economic and social ills. These results differ from the results of the consensus view (Configuration A), for which there was little variation in average percentages for the two periods. A comparison of Configurations A and B, the two contrasting discourse aggregates of *Fortune*'s view of the state, seems warranted, and thus, a discussion of these differences follows immediately after a description of the two discourse categories that comprise Configuration B.

Discourse Category #4, "The state's interference hinders growth and development; deregulation is advocated," emphasizes that business must operate in an environment free from governmental regulation. Articles claim that business is unable to efficiently and effectively allocate resources if the state regulates business, and interferes with business operations. Freedom to contract and competition in the marketplace (natural market forces) are promoted as forces superior to any state intervention or regulation. For example, in 1973, one article claims that the 1960s merger movement had a neutral effect on competition in the long run, and thus the Justice Department's antitrust division is accused of "attacking power per se" and "going far beyond its responsibility as an enforcement agency" (*Fortune*, April 1973, p. 70). This accusation contrasts discourses promoting the state's role in antitrust legislation as preserving the short-run interests of shareholders or employees.

Discourse Category #4 includes articles which accuse the state of not acting to control labor unions in contrast to discourses encouraging and supporting the state's negotiations and coalitions with labor. Characteristic of articles in discourse category #4, the state is accused of legislating inefficiencies and ill-conceived labor practices (*Fortune*, September 1973, p. 192), and thus elimination of government intervention and regulation is demanded.

Discourse Category #5, "Welfare state policies are critiqued as impediments to growth and oppressive to all social members," includes texts claiming that the state is irresponsible and inefficient, particularly concerning fiscal matters. The state's expenditures are discussed as detrimental to the economy and the nation's security, in contrast to a view that state expenditures enhance economic and social development. Transfer payments and social programs are referred to as an oppressive, redundant bureaucracy and discussed in terms of causing society's ills, rather than preventing or diffusing them. Additionally, government subsidies to business are critiqued as unnecessary in that it is not the state's role to protect businesses against competitive forces. Welfare policies are held responsible for causing unproductivity, inequities in the distribution of wealth, and other social ills.

Prior sections argued that in the early years of the 1960s the state was committed to maintaining economic growth and economic security by organizing alliances and serving as a mediator between various protagonists. However, these alliances unraveled as evidenced in the economic crises and social and political problems of the late 1960s and early 1970s. Therefore, we would expect that during the late 1960s there would be changing patterns of discourse concerning the state.

The increase in Configuration B, negative rhetoric regarding the state, coincides with the economic crises and social upheavals in the later years of our study. Increasingly, state intervention was blamed. The results are most striking between 1970 and 1973; during this period critiques against the state comprised 17.5 percent of the discourse in *Fortune*, almost twice the percentage devoted to support and celebration of the state. This illustrates the mutability of discursive practice. In the early period of the study it makes sense to view society in terms of consensus, the state "means" protection, and is a partner in achieving shared objectives. However, in the later years of the study a different form of meaning is increasingly given commonsense status—a view which cherishes the freedom of the marketplace over the protective role of the state.

During the early years of the Seventies when business profits begin to decline, there is a clarion call to deregulate the marketplace and release business from the hindrance of government interference. These discourses represent 14.5 percent, 16.5 percent, 22 percent, and 13.5 percent of our coding of Fortune in the years 1970 through 1973. Also note that in the 1970–1973 period the total percentage of *Fortune* devoted to the state is at its highest average, almost 27 percent.

The complexity of the relationship between the two discursive configurations of the state is illustrated by the following articles that appeared in the post-1970 period. In an article that appeared in July 1972, the claim was made that "clearly businessmen have lost much of their old aversion to close ties with government. Many feel threatened from several directions these days—from foreign competitors, environmentalists, and consumer advocates—and they tend to look upon government as an ally" (*Fortune*, July 1972, p. 41). The article noted that laissez faire attitudes had receded, in that businessmen did not strongly object to the state's implementation of wage-price controls. A second article in the same issue called for state involvement in determining which overseas markets were conducive to American business success (p. 61). As an illustration of the second discursive configuration, in the same issue *Fortune* accused the state's overzealous regulatory agencies with "overcontrolling" merchandising and product development (p. 70).

These examples illustrate that as a part of the ongoing process of reconstituting the conditions necessary for reproducing the social order, business discourse concerning the state undergoes transformations. One explanation of the simultaneous occurrence of different discursive themes is that in transition periods there are changing relations of force in the political class struggle, a shifting of ideological configurations, and a changing balance between the state apparatuses. Hall et al. (1978) describe the 1970s as a period of shift from hegemony of consensus to hegemony of coercion. But the period is an arrangement of themes that overlap because of "structurally different forces developing at different tempos and rhythms" (Hall et al., 1978, p. 219). Thus, we observe an interweaving of the discourses which give social life its meaning.

Fortune Configuration C

Configuration C combines five discourse categories promoting the benevolent manner in which managers conduct business. Business objectives are viewed as community objectives because they benefit all social members. In particular, pursuing profits is seen as natural, enhancing the life of employees (rather than compromising their interests). Interactions within organizations are viewed harmoniously, emphasizing managers' creativity, dynamic personalities, and personable actions toward employees. The growth of private business is applauded for its positive contribution in increasing wealth, and therefore, increasing the welfare of the public and the entire nation. Articles in Configuration C claim that the involvement of wealthy individuals in politics is commendable and does not jeopardize the independence or benevolence of government. These industrial statespersons are concerned with equality and rights for all members of society. Configuration C's attributes will be referred to as the "consensual view of society and the business community."

Table VII
FORTUNE **CONFIGURATION C:**
A consensual view of society and business,
emphasizing shared, community objectives.

Percentages Devoted to Configuration C:

1960–1966	19.6%
1967–1973	<u>15.9%</u>
Decrease	3.7%

Discourses in this configuration include:

♦ Managers and the wealthy benefiting society as industrial statespersons and philanthropists;

♦ Praise for managerial insights, creativity, and leadership in organizations;

♦ Pursuit of profit is universally beneficial;

♦ Praising domestic growth for its benefits to all social members;

♦ People's capitalism: widespread ownership ensures managers are responsive to society.

Referring to Table VII, the results indicate that during 1960 through 1966, Configuration C represented 19.6 percent of the discourse in *Fortune*; for the period 1967 through 1973, the percentage drops to 15.9 percent (a decline of 3.7 percent). The decrease in the percentage of Configuration C is more striking in the later years using a different periodization framework. When we combine the period of 1960 through 1969, Configuration C represents 20.4 percent of the discourse, but declines to 11.2 percent in the period of 1970 through 1973, a decrease of 9.2 percent. Although a percentage of 11.2 percent reflects that *Fortune* is continuing to devote articles to Configuration C in the 1970 through 1973 period, it is only slightly more than half the 20.4 percent average for the previous period. Individually, the five discourse categories in this configuration describe different aspects of managers, employees, stockholders, customers, and state officials. The categories, however, are linked by their portrayal of business as imbued with benevolence and a belief in compromise. An analysis of the five discourses individually indicates a decline in each of these categories over the period.

The decline in the literature's emphasis on social harmony, well-intentioned managers, mediation, and compromise reflects a decrease in consensual discourses. Once again, discursive patterns are demonstrated to be mutable, and these changes illustrate that economic, social, and political practices, or crises can be re-constituted. Relying less on discourses promoting the benevolence of managers and profits reflects a failure of this strategy in achieving cohesion in society. In turn, the decline in these discourses suggests that the future cohesion of society will be managed by other strategies. An examination of Configuration D, which follows, offers some insight into these changing strategies.

Fortune Configuration D

Configuration D is a view of the world of business, and the interaction of business and society, in terms of competitive tactics in the struggle for survival. Articles naturalize competition between individuals in the harsh environment of business where strategic maneuvering, subtle undermining of the competition, and cunning interventions prevail as the natural order of business affairs. "It's a jungle out there" and managers who dutifully implement these schemes are to be praised. There is deference to existing hierarchies, structure, order, and control embedded in the status quo. By promoting obedience to management authority and compliance with managerial decisions these articles reflect a rhetoric of support for enduring institutional structures and conformity. Discussions concerning social responsibility of business are in terms of survival and legitimation, one article suggesting "it makes good economic sense." It is the incessant market order that mandates corporate behavior, not a concern for society's well-being as an ideal, or aspiration for protecting the public. In Configuration D, the metaphor for society is survival of the fittest, and the ends justify the means.

Included in this view is the promotion of individualistic pursuits as an intrinsic part of the free enterprise system, and suggestions that the future progress of society rests on self-reliance, and concern for the self. Articles claim that it is inherent for members of society to pursue their individual objectives first and foremost (in contrast to a concern for the collective good). Frequently, individualism is discussed synonymously with freedom, security, and dignity, disregarding that race, sex, access to property, and education often "stack the deck" at the outset. Success is measured in terms of acquiring and accumulating possessions (i. e., commodity fetishism). There is a sense of intensity in the articles' portrayal of society's desire for accumulating material goods. Configuration D will be referred to as the "survival view of society and the business community."

Table VIII
Fortune **Configuration D:**
Celebrating individualistic and competitive aspects of society
and the business community, and the will to survive.

Percentages Devoted to Configuration D:

1960–1966	28.8%
1967–1973	33.2%
Increase	4.4%

Discourses in this configuration include:

♦ Social Darwinism in society and business, as in nature, results in survival of the fittest;
♦ Encouraging individualism;
♦ Promotion of material wealth as a measure of success;
♦ Management planning and authority is essential;
♦ Monopolies and oligopolies are improvements in competition;
♦ Economic rationality justifies corporate concern for social improvements;
♦ Labor strikes are subject to the harsh realities of the market.

In the periodization analysis, Configuration D shows an increase of 4.4 percent. Using a different break point, Configuration D increases from an average of 29.1 percent in the 1960 through 1969 period to an average of 35.9 percent for the 1970 through 1973 period, which is an increase of 6.8 percent. It is during this latter period of the study, characterized as an economic slump, that an increasing prevalence of discourses emphasizing competition and the survival of the fittest occurs. Note, however, that throughout the entire period there is a predominance in Configuration D discourses; the range of 29.1 percent to 35.9 percent indicates that one-third of *Fortune*'s discourses are devoted to these themes.

What are the features of Configuration D that would explain the increase in the latter period of the study? Do the above results have any relationship to other discourses in the study? The answers to these questions are combined below, with a further interpretation of the results and additional summary data.

The increase in *Fortune*'s promotion of Configuration D coincides with a decline of Configuration C. Referring back to the discourses in Configuration C, they present a consensual and harmonious view of society and the business community, in contradistinction to the harsh portrayal of the social order in Configuration D. Yet Configurations C and D do share attributes and commonalities in that both are ideological themes concerned with the relationship between business and society.

Both promote business and the pursuit of profit and show cohesiveness in a society organized through a profit motive. It is this attribute of ideology that Althusser (1971) referred to as the social cement, or common sense—the ability of ideology to make sense of the world around us, and by shaping this understanding, its ability to influence and mold social acts and practices. By portraying a social order embraced by managerial insight, business leadership, and profit as natural, universal, and the best of all possible worlds, social structures are uncontested. Both configurations share in their mediation and obfuscation of the social conflicts underlying the social practices and framework of the society.

However, cohesion is installed through quite different strategies in the two discursive aggregates. Configuration C's community view, promoting harmony and consensus in organizational life contrasts Configuration D's celebration of corporate hierarchy, efficiency, competition, and survival of the fittest. Configuration D asserts that in the social and economic world only the fittest survive, and thus the discourse justifies numerous tactics that might appear harsh (Bluestone and Hamson, 1982).

Configuration D rises to a peak of 35.9 percent during the early Seventies, a period of decreasing profits, increasing inflation, rising unemployment, and an economic environment of international competition. One explanation of this decline is that it no longer makes sense to promote the harmonious and cooperative workings of society and business, when, increasingly, the partnership between labor and business has broken down, profit rates have declined, unemployment is high, etc. Configuration C, the consensus view, appears to be replaced, in part, with Configuration D. Cohesion in society as socio-economic-political life practices is increasingly viewed in terms that are justifiably and quite naturally more coercive than consensual. The message that increases with the increase in Configuration D is that the business community cannot be expected to assist in social harmony during a period of harsh economic realities; businesses must concern themselves with their own survival. If we combine the survival discourse with the increasing critique of the state's benevolence (Configuration B), *Fortune's* discourse increasingly reflects the authoritarian and coercive ideology characteristic of a hegemony of coercion (Hall et al., 1978).

Fortune Configuration E

Configuration E is an aggregate of discourse directed at international issues. Portraying an image of the United States as a protector of other nations against threatening forces, these discourses promote the maintenance of the United States as a powerful nation. The task of industrializing other countries and promoting American business interests is conveyed as an natural hallmark of modernization and development. Articles in this configuration are nationalistic, encouraging American business to think in terms of American objectives and goals when investing in foreign countries.

Table IX
***Fortune* Configuration E:**
Championing American interests, values, and business practices in international affairs.

Percentages Devoted to Configuration E:

1960–1966	13.6%
1967–1973	12.4%
Decrease	1.2%

Discourses in this configuration include:

♦ It is natural for the United States to compete internationally for markets and further capital accumulation;

♦ The United States' international role as a powerful protector is vital to ensuring freedom and preventing communist threat;

♦ Market capitalism is a benevolent force throughout the world.

The results indicate very little change in this configuration. Overall, the average is between 13.6 percent and 12.4 percent. A more detailed analysis of the three component categories (#18, #19, and #20) also indicates a consistency throughout the period.

Discourse Category #18, "It is natural for the United States to compete internationally for markets and further capital accumulation," is illustrated in the following article appearing in *Fortune*. The article suggests that because of the low inflation rate and high growth, investment in Mexico looks like a good opportunity. However, the article warns U.S. companies to proceed cautiously, one reason being that "poverty is too widespread to provide adequate markets for much large-scale industry" (*Fortune*, September 1965). Such statements emphasize the positive influence of market rationality, commercialization, and

U.S. corporate growth, neglecting the socio-economic problems of poverty and its relation to global intervention, international industry and U.S. penetration. The decision to invest abroad is posed unproblematically in terms of profit strategies for American business; it is not a decision based on the needs or culture of the inhabitants of the host country.

The economic-directed characteristic of Discourse Category #18 also appears in an article entitled, "The Goods of War Pour Out" (*Fortune*, March 1966). This article states that the biggest threat to the South Vietnamese economy is inflation, exacerbated by the United States' "spending GIs" and the bidding up of wages due to military construction. But the evidence is that American determination to stand by South Vietnam gives confidence instead of inflationary panic. Consequently, the United States has an opportunity to benefit by the natural and financial resources South Vietnam has to offer, i.e., "the goods of war pour out."

One component of Configuration E is the idealizing of capitalism in general, praised for its global benefits, materially and socially (Discourse Category #20). To illustrate, one article indicates there should be optimism concerning the economic development and future of underdeveloped countries because they are taking a more "encouraging attitude toward private investment" (*Fortune*, October 1966). This statement equates private investment with future benefits for underdeveloped countries; foreign investment is associated with a desired evolutionary stage for developing countries, offering expanding mechanization, secularization, and urbanization. An alternative perspective is omitted, namely that economic and cultural interdependencies, expansions, and integration are encroachments into these countries with little reason for optimism that these countries will be the beneficiaries.

Overall, the international discourse remained consistent in terms of percentage and its components. The percentage of *Fortune* devoted to Configuration E was, on average, 13 percent. The events during this period included a range of international controversies for the United States such as the Cold War, the Vietnam war, the economic achievements of Japan, and so on. Discourses regarding these matters appeared throughout *Fortune* at a fairly steady, significant average of 13 percent.

A detailed analysis of Configuration E indicates that of the three discourse categories, Discourse Category #18 is the greatest contributor, i.e., has the highest average percentage of the three discourse categories in the configuration. Discourse Category #18 advocates that "it is natural for the United States to compete internationally for markets and further capital accumulation." This illustrates the consistency in views on competition, both internationally and domestically, that cohesion in society depends on advocating and respecting the marketplace, competition, and the growth of capital. The choice of issues to discuss regarding international affairs is directed, most frequently, in terms of investment, competition, and an American company's concern for ensuring a dominant stake in available foreign investments.

Discourses that are ignored, repressed, and silenced are often more significant than discourses that are undertaken. There is rarely any discussion in *Fortune* of the ethnocentricity in foreign relations or that free market regimes may not be universally desirable for all cultures, societies, and so on. The transformation of family roles, strains on traditional forms of kinship and mutual support, and the pervasive phenomena of female subordination are the common experience of communities upon the entry of U.S. multinationals; yet these images are rarely depicted in *Fortune*. Advocating global cooperation without concern for market rationality would be one alternative to Fortune's perspective; for *Fortune*, however, it is natural to look at the world and see one great marketplace.

Fortune Configuration F

In this configuration science and technological advancements are praised for their economic and social benefits. Research is promoted and celebrated because new discoveries (e.g., new products) are what profits are made of; research is a strategy for generating profits. Additionally, new technologies are depicted as beneficial for the entire economy, by increasing U.S. competition in new production processes and global markets, and by potentially decreasing costs of the factors of production.

Although the percentage of texts concerning Configuration F averages approximately 14.8 percent during the earlier years of the study, the results indicate a decrease in the later years.

Included in Configuration F are descriptions of the marvels of science and that science may indeed be the answer to solving social ills such as overpopulation or environmental degradation such as pollution. These romanticized views of science's capabilities in solving social problems obscure the underlying causes and social choices surrounding these issues. Pollution may be viewed as an externality that corporations knowingly could prevent but impose on the broader society to resolve. Similarly, the larger questions of poverty and the global distribution of wealth is fundamental to overpopulation phenomena, yet *Fortune* limits the discourse to the omnipotence of science. The potential for solving these problems through scientific advancement is severely limited without attention to these more essential issues.

Table X
Fortune **Configuration F:**
Omnipotence of science, technology, computers.

Percentages Devoted to Configuration F:

1960–1966	14.8%
1967–1973	11.0%
Decrease	3.8%

Discourses in this configuration include:
♦ Omnipotence of science, technology;
♦ Omnipotence of computers in particular.

Another aspect of this configuration is that science is considered neutral, and is depoliticized; this contrasts discourses viewing science and the choice of scientific questions as socially constituted. Scientific research is beset with hierarchies, authoritative controls, and norms that delimit what is acceptable research inquiry, challenging any notion of scientific objectivity within the scientific community (as we saw in Chapter III). Scientific inquiry has undergone scrutiny by feminist theorists for its predisposition toward male perspectives, focuses, and behaviors, ignoring objects of research, participants, and topics of interest to women (French, 1986; Gilligan, 1982; Haraway, 1989; Jaggar, 1983; Lerner, 1986). This critique extends to the very nature of the search for knowledge, and the basic foundations of what we call science. These theorists argue that contemporary scientific inquiry privileges ways of knowing and discovery that maintain structures of male dominance—that truth is produced in the interest of those with the power and the desire to shape reality for their own interests. The social constitutiveness of knowledge, including racial prejudices, gender biases, class characteristics, and cultural restraints, precludes a separation of nature, science, and inquiry as to make objective knowledge possible.

The neutrality and global benevolence of science and technology is illustrated in the sharing of ideas that the West and East promote, specifically, that science is a communal activity. Additionally, Configuration F argues that the benefits of scientific knowledge are equally distributed among all people, and implies that the advancements of American scientists' research are equally relevant and beneficial to other cultures.

The results in Table X indicate that during the early part of the study, 1960 through 1967, the omnipotence of science was, on average, 14.8%. During these years of the boom period, businesses would be expected to have greater discretion concerning research and development in contrast to a period of declining profits. The decrease in Configuration F discourses is most prominent in the later years, when economic conditions were deteriorating. Throughout the entire portion, the discourse related to computers only averaged less than 3 percent.

It appears that in the years of the slump, discourses were less inclined to promote a quick fix type of strategy for increasing profits (e.g., through new products). Rather, other discourses were increasingly promoted, for example, appeals for deregulation (Configuration A) and promotion of efficiency and control for the survival of business (Configuration D). Scientific advancements and knowledge are less likely to be marveled at during harsh economic periods.

Fortune Configuration G: Miscellaneous and Sundry

This category is informative in assessing that which is repressed, excluded, denied, ignored, or limited in the arena of discursive practices—it possesses significance by exclusion. Configuration G is a grouping of miscellaneous discourses averaging 5 percent over the period. As there was little change, no summary of results is reported in a separate table. Categories in this configuration include, for example, education and philosophy (e.g., "What are ideas?"), and managerial greed and corruption (not justified in terms of survival, the theme of Configuration D). Also discussed, but barely so, was the accounting profession. Articles on accounting included a description of the growing services that the larger auditing firms now provide and the need for relevant information from financial statements. (Although a separate accounting category was developed, the discourse is clearly interrelated with other discourse categories.) The area of business ethics and the related discourse on accounting ethics is noticeable by its exclusion and is discussed in more detail in the accounting discussion, specifically Accounting Configuration M.

This concludes the presentation of the twenty-five discourse categories and seven configurations for *Fortune* magazine.

Discursive Activity of the Accounting Journals

This section describes the results of examining the accounting literature, and incorporates throughout a comparison with *Fortune*'s discourse. Table XI [see following page] summarizes the average percentages for the six Configurations, H through N, of the accounting discourses for the fourteen-year period of study. These results are also described in detail for each configuration.

Accounting Configuration H

Configuration H includes texts promoting and praising self-regulation of the profession. Given the profession's expertise in financial reporting matters, these articles assert that rule making and standard setting should be the mandate of the accounting profession, and that the role of the SEC and other state agencies should be limited to an oversight function. In addition to the profession's superior ability over state organizations, advantages emerging from autonomy include professional independence and objectivity. Direct governmental intervention is ill-advised, as accountants can be relied upon to act professionally, respond to user's needs, craft appropriate standards, and reap the efficacy of self-regulation. In other words, autonomy from the state is common sense—an optimal form of regulation for society.

Table XI
Discursive Activity of the *Journal of Accountancy* (JA) and *Accounting Review* (AR)
1960-1973

	Discourse Category #	JA %	AR %	AVE %
Accounting Configuration H: Critique of	26	11.3	7.9	9.6
state intervention and promotion of self-	27	9.4	4.0	6.7
regulation and praise of accountants'	28	12.6	9.3	10.9
professionalism.	29	7.8	8.0	7.9
		41.1%	29.2%	35.1%
Accounting Configuration J:	30	10.1	13.3	11.7
Accounting benefits business and society	31	3.1	16.1	9.6
by assisting in the efficient allocation	32	3.1	8.4	5.8
of resources and economic growth.		16.3%	37.8%	27.1%
Accounting Configuration K: The profes-	33	6.0	0.8	3.4
sion is devoted to protecting the public; this	34	11.1	5.9	8.5
is a natural role, ensured by the independ-	35	8.0	4.0	6.0
ence of the profession, and enhanced by	36	4.9	2.1	3.5
accountants' ethical nature and commitment.		30.0%	12.8%	21.4%
Accounting Configuration L: Advocating	37	0.0	9.8	4.9
statistical and accounting expertise in	38	4.1	5.1	4.6
developing CIS.		4.1%	14.9%	9.5%
Accounting Configuration M: Promoting				
the international benefits of accounting;	39	1.6	0.2	0.9
praising its contribution to economic and	40	1.2	0.5	0.8
social freedom, international trade and	41	2.1	0.7	1.4
competition, and global democracy.		4.9%	1.4%	3.1%
Accounting Configuration N:				
Sundry Discourses	#42,#43	4.0%	3.2%	3.6%
Total Percent (Rounded to 100%)		100.0%	100.0%	100.0%

Table XII
Accounting Configuration H:
Critique of state intervention and promotion of self-regulation; praise of accountants' professionalism.

Percentages Devoted to Configuration H:

1960/61–1966/67	29.2%
1967/68–1973/74	41.6%
Increase	12.4%

Discourse categories in this configuration include:
♦ Self-regulation is superior to state intervention;
♦ Support for the authoritative institutions and mechanisms of the profession;
♦ Accounting is responsive to financial statement users;
♦ Professionalism ensures limited regulation is universally beneficial.

Note: The presentation of dual years reflects a one year lag for the *Accounting Review*.

The results indicate that throughout the late Sixties and early Seventies the discourses comprising Configuration H were increasing. By the later years, 41.6 percent of the two accounting publications were devoted to this discourse—almost half of the accounting literature. Throughout the entire period of study, this rhetoric comprises a significant proportion of the accounting discourse, an average of 35.4 percent over all years. Given the configuration's prominence, how does it illustrate accounting's participation in social conflict?

Configuration H is an opportunity to study the profession's negotiations with the state and the general strategies used in conflicts arising with the state. This strategy is one of advocating self-rule and freedom to form its own disclosure regulations without government intervention.

Within this discursive grouping are articles defensively promoting the importance, efficiency, and optimality of accounting autonomy in standard setting. Portraying itself as an open forum when standards and policy decisions are formulated, the profession claims a balanced responsiveness to various users (Discourse Category #28) and a neutrality in deliberations, an attribute the state is unable to achieve. Always seeking progress and improvement, the profession delves into the essence of (conflicting) needs of users, interrogating their interests and the diversity of their objectives, and aspires to respond with relevant information. These unique characteristics imbue the profession with a crucial role to society—useful, desirable, progress-seeking regulation.

Contrasting the high regard for accounting communicated in these articles, authors frequently insist that government involvement impairs society and business. A characteristic of Discourse Category #26, "Self-regulation is superior to state intervention," is the claim that government intervention causes misunderstandings between the public and business. For example, it is argued that the state misuses accounting terminology, confusing the investing public and generating inefficiencies in the marketplace.

In Discourse Category #27, "Support for the authoritative institutions and mechanisms of the profession," organizational and regulatory achievements are idealized. Generally accepted accounting principles (GAAP) are considered the culmination of experienced accountants deciding on the best possible standards of the highest possible quality. Internal regulations of its own members are also praised for their high standards, ensuring professional quality. Articles in this category argue that the conscientious application of self-policing standards justifies autonomy from the state. The scrupulous and meticulous effort of the profession to police its members ensures integrity without government intervention.

The increase in the rhetoric applicable to Configuration H mirrors changing discourse in the broader business community. As illustrated in the previous analysis of *Fortune*, during the later years we find business increasingly rejecting state interference. Articles in *Fortune*, portraying state regulations as dysfunctional to the economy and to society (*Fortune* Configuration B), increased 6.8 percent in the 1970–1973 period. *Fortune*'s expanding critique of the state coincides with the accounting profession's growing claim that the state should not interfere with accounting standard setting (Figure 1).

It appears that one reaction to this period's social conflicts is to concentrate on accounting's own legitimation and survival.

Figure 1
Journal of Accountancy*, *Accounting Review*, and *Fortune
Comparisons: Configuration H and Discourse #4

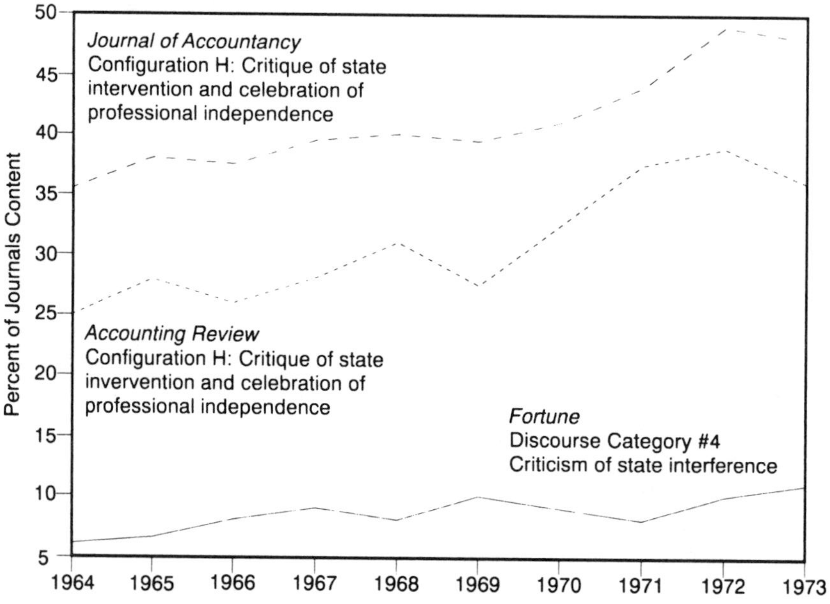

Journal of Accountancy
Configuration H: Critique of state intervention and celebration of professional independence

Accounting Review
Configuration H: Critique of state invervention and celebration of professional independence

Fortune
Discourse Category #4
Criticism of state interference

The profession's response to the economic crises of the early Seventies is to praise and advocate its quasi-independence from the state, and reject the state as a conflict resolver. By disenfranchising itself from the state, the profession asserts its special role in conflict resolution. In contrast to other state agencies, it encourages management and others to participate in the standard-setting process. This is one strategy by which the profession can maintain its status as a regulatory authority, while at the same time establish the profession's responsibility and sensitivity to participants concerned with financial data (managers, financial analysts).

As is characteristic of all discursive practices, the profession's choice of discourse is a complex set of reactions to its environment, which consequently affects the environment. Why does the profession reject the role of the state in resolving conflicts, promoting itself instead as a regulator? This rhetoric may be more appealing to the business community, particularly if the profession can convince business that they share mutual objectives. Additionally, the claim that accounting is uniquely suited to determining standards (due to objectivity, etc.) suggests society is best served with the profession free to set regulations, thus directing discourse toward its own survival. In promoting its own organization as superior to state intervention, Configuration H forms a social cohesion similar to the ideologies of *Fortune*. Increasingly what is made to make sense in the authoritarian regime of the Seventies is less trust in the state and a concern for survival.

A detailed analysis of Configuration H indicates that Discourse Category #27, "Support for the authoritative institutions and mechanisms of the profession," was a substantial portion of the 1970–1973 increase; it contributed 65 percent to the increase. Thus, during the early 1970s there is a growing proportion of the professional literature that presents the organizational apparatus as one of cooperation, efficiency, and professionalism. Discourse Category #27 praises the profession's self-policing structure for its ability to ensure integrity without state regulation.

Why is this particular discourse category increasing so substantially during this period? One possible explanation concerns the difficult relationship between accounting and Congress during this period with the above discourse serving as the profession's defense. Congressional investigations and hearings questioned whether the profession's disclosure rules were effective in preventing financial manipulation and fraud (resulting in the subsequent Moss and Metcalf investigations in 1976 and 1977). In addition, the profession was being criticized for its inadequate standards in maintaining its own independence in the external audit process. During the early years of the Seventies there were numerous internal re-evaluations of the profession's rule-making apparatus. The profession formed its own committees for self-appraisal: the Wheat Committee (1971), the Trueblood Committee (1971), and the Cohen Commission (1974).

One of the outcomes of these conflicts was the dismantling of its prior rule-making board, the Accounting Principles Board (APB) (which had been subject to much of the external criticism described above), and the establishment of the Financial Accounting Standards Board (FASB). In addition, the American Institute of Certified Public Accountants (AICPA) found it necessary to commission a Study Group on the Objectives of Financial Statements (1971–1973) in order to establish a broad framework for improving financial disclosures. The study was viewed as part of a continuing search for a formal set of objectives for the profession, and promised to provide insight and increased understanding concerning accounting's role in society.

Another potential factor that would increase discourses promoting internal cooperation is an external pressure resulting from labor shortages. During the latter part of our study, shortages in the profession and the strains on recruiting were exacerbated. The Department of Labor projected in a 1971 report that 33,000 accountants would be needed each year through 1980, but only 16,000 students with accounting backgrounds were expected to graduate in 1971. Cooperation within the profession is necessary to promote a good image in recruiting students and in retaining accountants in the profession. Government regulators might claim that labor shortages provide proof of a disorganized profession and that labor shortages strain the profession's abilities to serve. Thus, as a self-preservation strategy, the profession promotes to outsiders an image of cooperation and effectiveness within the profession.

Comparison of the Accounting Journals: Configuration H

On average, over all years, both journals devote a significant portion to Configuration H. However, the *Journal of Accountancy* exhibits a greater concern for these state and organizational discourses. For the entire 1960–1973 period, the *Journal of Accountancy* devotes 41.1 percent to Configuration H; the *Accounting Review*'s percentage is 29.2 percent.

The periodization analysis also indicates differences between the journals. The *Journal of Accountancy* increases its percentage 11.4 percent, to an average of 49.1 percent, in the 1970–1973 period. Almost half of the *Journal of Accountancy* editorials are devoted to discourses in Configuration H in this period. The *Accounting Review* percentage increases 8 percent over the 1970–1973 period, to 35.7 percent. Thus, in the 1970–1973 period, the *Journal of Accountancy* devotes 13.4 percent more than the *Accounting Review* to these discourses. See Figure 2.

Upon further analysis, we note that the greatest difference between the journals in this period is due to the Discourse

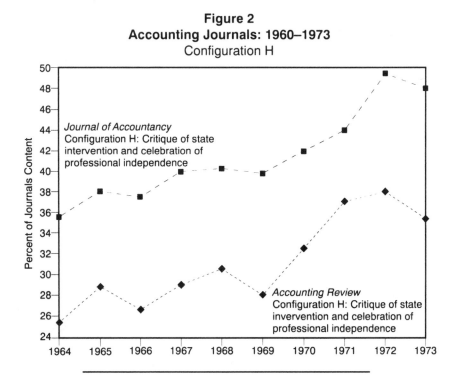

Figure 2
Accounting Journals: 1960–1973
Configuration H

Category #27, "Support for the authoritative institutions and mechanisms of the profession." Articles in this category emphasize organizational planning, coordination, and effectiveness. In the 1970–1973 period, the *Journal of Accountancy* devotes 19.6 percent of its editorials to Discourse Category #27—almost one-fifth of the editorials. In contrast, the category represents only 2.8 percent of the *Accounting Review* during the 1970–1973 period.

This difference may reflect the *Journal of Accountancy*'s public relations orientation, or it may reflect its affiliation with the American Institute of Certified Public Accountants. The *Journal of Accountancy* claims that its editorials are not pontifications of the professional bodies, rather, they are meant to call attention to matters which deserve attention from the accounting profession. The review of editorials indicates an increasing concern for professional authority and increased promotion of organizational planning, Discourse Category #27. Although the *Journal of Accountancy* devoted, on average, 5.3 percent of its editorials to Discourse Category #27 in the period 1960–1969, the percentage expands almost fourfold, to 19.6 percent, of all editorials from 1970 through 1973.

Why, then, was the *Journal of Accountancy* so substantially concerned with coordination between accountants, and control within the organizational machinery (the APB and the FASB)? It is speculated that the difficult environment for the profession, including increasing external pressure from the state, a tight labor market, and declining profits, all contributed to the *Journal of Accountancy*'s emphasis on internal discipline, self-reform, and self-evaluation in order to combat external pressures more effectively.

The results illustrate shifting discourse patterns during the period and their influence on knowledge and practice in the public sphere. When the *Journal of Accountancy* advocates an appreciation of the accounting profession's self-rule, this becomes a way of viewing the profession as quasi-independent from the state. Opportunities to observe the profession's discourse while under congressional investigation emerge in different eras, and in 1985 the Dingell Commission, a congressional oversight committee, began scrutinizing, once again, the question of independence in the accounting profession. The results of the study here offer a framework for examining the profession's discursive reaction to conflict with the state in the early Seventies. Similar or different discourses may be emphasized and advocated as part of changing pressures and crises.

Accounting Configuration J

Articles in Configuration J present profit maximization as an inherent, common, and endemic objective of accounting, business, and society; it is universally desirable because it preserves economic well-being for all social members. Included in this configuration are articles equating domestic growth (e.g., industrial growth) with economic prominence, technological supremacy, and productivity advancements paramount to social well-being. Growth is progress, the hallmark of modernization, perceived as a unifying aspiration for the broad social world. Articles in Configuration J underscore that markets are synchronized, mutually adjusting, and coordinated owing to accounting's role: accountants are expert custodians of the information required to fine tune the system. By disseminating the information in a timely manner, accounting insures optimal economic activity is achieved by managers, benefiting society as a whole. Accounting's role in maintaining market mechanisms is crucial because the information provided by accountants (e.g., financial statements) is central to ensuring a self-equilibrating, productive, and cooperative marketplace.

Table XIII
Accounting Configuration J:
Accounting benefits business and society by assisting
in the efficient allocation of resources and economic growth.

Percentages Devoted to Configuration J:

1960/61–1966/67	32.2%
1967/68–1973/74	21.9%
Decrease	10.3%

Discourse categories in this configuration include:
♦ Assisting business is a benevolent responsibility of the accounting profession;
♦ The efficient allocation of resources is a common objective for society in which accounting plays a crucial role;
♦ Domestic growth is universally beneficial; accounting contributes toward this goal.

Note: The presentation of dual years reflects a one year lag for the *Accounting Review*.

Also characteristic of articles in Configuration J is confidence, assurances, and faith in the net income figure as a reliable measure of business performance and as a significant tool in managerial and investor decisions. It is instrumental in the efficient allocation of resources. It follows that since accountants are responsible for attesting to net income numbers, the profession facilitates in this mutually beneficent allocation. Authors maintain that society prospers when stockholders, the marketplace, and business enterprises are promoted and strengthened. The common viewpoint running through Configuration J is the coherence and accord of the marketplace and the progress that is derived from business.

The results in Table XIII indicate a decline of Configuration J in the later years of the study. From an average peak of 32.2 percent, in 1960–1966, to a low of 21.9 percent in 1967–1973, the decrease is 10.3 percent.

Why does this configuration represent a smaller proportion of accounting literature in the latter period of the study? What factors coincide with the changing rhetoric of a decreasing view of the world in terms of the universal benefits of business, growth, and profits?

The decline corresponds to a period of decreasing profit rates for business, contrasting with the economic boom of the earlier years. The economic crisis in the late Sixties and early Seventies was met, as we saw in *Fortune*, with diminishing discourses celebrating mutually enhancing tendencies between society and business. The consensus view of society captured in *Fortune*'s Configuration C declines throughout the early Seventies, evidence that during harsh economic periods a desirable strategy is to lower expectations of harmonious relationships—it does not make sense to rely on the marketplace to achieve coherence and unity when profits are falling. Accounting participates in these antagonisms through its mutual assertion that there should be less reliance on the marketplace and economic growth to ensure social consensus and harmony.

Although there is a decline in Configuration J, an average of 22.5 percent continues to be devoted to these discourses in the 1970–1973 period in the accounting literature. This reflects that Configuration J is comprised of discourses that defend the importance of accounting—its useful role and purpose—in a capitalist society. Thus one article states, "The business accountant is a . . . custodian . . . of the profit mechanism that guides and controls our free enterprise system" (*Accounting Review*, January 1967, p. 2).

Articles in Discourse Category #30, "Assisting business is a benevolent responsibility of the accounting profession," describe accountants as dynamic professionals who understand the numerous complexities in financial and business matters and thus can contribute to the business objective of earning a profit. Conflicts of interest in serving business is disregarded insofar as profit maximization and growth are universalized as natural. Articles encourage the use of accounting procedures to assist business in avoiding taxes; neglected are the consequences: What are the effects on the state's tax revenues? Might they be problematic to the society in general? What are the implications for the distribution of wealth?

Another explanation of the decrease in these themes in the latter years of the study may be due to the following: during periods of prosperity the accounting profession emphasizes (advertises) its role in attaining good economic performance and growth; when profits decline, accounting can no longer boast that it has contributed to these achievements, thus these discourses decline. However, we would expect these discourses to be an important part of accounting literature in both favorable and unfavorable economic conditions since they present accounting as an important and integral part of business and economic well-being in general.

Comparison of the Accounting Journals: Configuration J

The journals contribute quite differently to the above results in terms of the overall period, the periodization analysis, and the discourse categories of this configuration. Overall, the *Accounting Review* emphasizes Configuration J to a greater extent than the *Journal of Accountancy*. For the overall period, 1960 through 1973, the *Accounting Review* devotes an average of 37.8 percent to Configuration J, which is over twice the percentage for the *Journal of Accountancy*—an average of 16.3 percent for the fourteen-year period. The greatest difference between the journals is in the 1970–1973 period. In these years an average of 8.1 percent of the editorials in the *Journal of Accountancy* are concerned with Configuration J. In contrast, over a fourfold difference—36.8 percent—is the percentage for the *Accounting Review*, representing over one-third of its feature articles. See Figure 3.

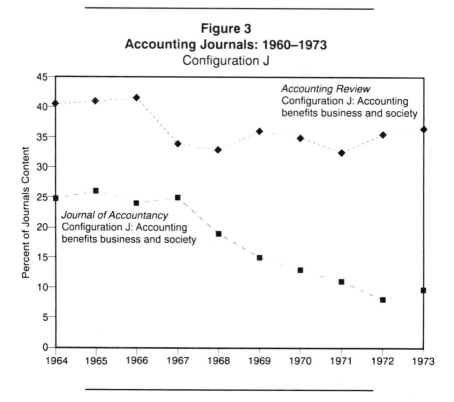

Figure 3
Accounting Journals: 1960–1973
Configuration J

In regard to the 1970 through 1973 period, one reason for the *Journal of Accountancy*'s small percentage (8.1 percent) in contrast to the results for the *Accounting Review* (36.8 percent) may be the public relations orientation of the *Journal of Accountancy* in contrast with the academic orientation of the *Accounting Review*. The *Journal of Accountancy* may be more concerned that it is inappropriate to celebrate harmony in the marketplace and praise accounting's contribution to business during a period of falling profits, e.g., the early Seventies. Thus, although the *Journal of Accountancy* concentrated 23 percent of its editorials on Configuration J in the 1960–1966 boom period, this percentage drops to 8.1 percent in the 1970–1973 slump period. However, the *Accounting Review*, as a research journal, displays less concern for these public relations strategies. The results for the

Accounting Review indicate that during the 1960–1966 period, 41.4 percent of the feature articles concern this configuration; the percentage for the 1970–1973 period is 36.8 percent. Although the percentage declines, the *Accounting Review* continues to devote over one-third of its feature articles to this configuration in the latter period.

One category in Configuration J, "The efficient allocation of resources is a natural objective for society in which accounting plays a crucial role," (Discourse Category #31), receives a score of 20.6 percent during the 1970–1973 period. This means one-fifth of the *Accounting Review* feature articles are devoted to this singular category, #31. In Discourse Category #31, authors claim a proper measure of income is crucial in achieving an efficient allocation of resources, and thus, category #31 is comprised of articles attempting to find the best measure of income.

Why is there such a high proportion of this category in the *Accounting Review* during this period? Above, it was speculated that the *Accounting Review*, as an academic, research-oriented journal, may be less sensitive to, or less affected by, the economic condition of declining profits in the early Seventies from a public relations viewpoint. The *Accounting Review*'s concern for establishing the best technique for measuring income and economic efficiency coincides with "the dawning of capital markets research in finance, and the propagation of methods first developed in the literatures of psychology and sociology" (Zeff [editor], *Accounting Review*, 1978, p. 470). With new techniques available, the above findings (a concentration on measurement) may be interpreted as a prelude, or a confirmation, of the recent appraisal by the editor of the *Accounting Review* that the "wave of rigor" in the accounting literature results in research that is overly narrow (Zeff, *Accounting Review*, 1978, 1983).

The concentration on measurement of income (Discourse Category #31) in the 1970–1973 period may demonstrate that accounting researchers concentrate on small questions, rather than tackling big ones (Williams, 1985). One concern of this study is to consider future and potential roles of accounting and accounting research. Therefore, the claim that accounting researchers are myopic in their perceptions of research questions, thus limiting the development of knowledge, is crucial in considering future directions of accounting. The results of the research data above—a narrow concentration in academic research—

illustrate a lack of reflection by accounting researchers, i.e., that there are other questions to be asked.

Accounting Configuration K

Articles in Configuration K appeal to idealistic, higher values of the profession, portraying it as an ethical discipline, concerned, ultimately, with serving the public. Reflecting admirable images of the profession's responsibility to society, this discourse reveals aspirations of moral commitment, integrity, and social desirability. "Independence" is given a special status in this discursive realm—it symbolizes the high ideal and purity of the accounting professional, recognizing issues of conflicts of interests, ethics, rights, and the need to take a moral stance.

Table XIV
Accounting Configuration K:

The profession is devoted to protecting the public interest; this is a natural role, ensured by the independence of the profession, and enhanced by accountants' ethical nature and personal commitment.

Percentages Devoted to Configuration K:

1960/61–1966/67	22.1%
1967/68–1973/74	20.8%
Decrease	1.3%

Discourses in this configuration include:
♦ The profession celebrates its ethical practices;
♦ Accountants have a natural ability to serve as public statespersons;
♦ Accountants' independence ensures third-party protection;
♦ Protecting the interests of accountants also protects society.

Note: The presentation of dual years reflects a one year lag for the *Accounting Review*.

As the investing public relies upon the independent appraisal of accountants in making investment decisions, the profession is charged with protecting these individuals from deficiencies in reporting or from negligent internal control procedures. This responsibility is taken very seriously; it is reflected in the codifications, generally accepted accounting principles, standards, and regulations that accountants must adhere to in preparing and auditing financial information. Compelling proof of this responsibility exists in the profession's code of ethics where ethical standards of behavior, moral rectitude, and virtue are extolled; divergencies are condemned and punishable. Articles in Configuration K insist, however, that ethical practices are a natural inclination and characteristic of accountants at all times. The code of ethics is portrayed as a formality, giving the public additional assurances that their interests and rights are protected.

A common theme in Configuration K is a high regard for the independence of external auditors who review the financial statements of publicly held corporations. The characteristic of independence is portrayed as crucial in protecting the investing public because it increases the likelihood that misrepresentations in financial statements will be discovered and corrected. Independence, the articles insist, is a unique protective shield for the public; it ensures quality in financial reports, that the best interests of users are being served, and that broad social interests are advocated.

Accounting's role in serving society is conveyed by reference to the accountant's natural role in public policy decisions. Articles claim that accountants, as experts in financial matters, are ideally suited for assisting local and national governments in solving a wide range of financial problems and allocating state resources. Thus, the overall message of articles in Configuration K is that accountants are committed, virtuous, and principled servants of the public.

The empirical data summarized in Table XIV indicates a slight decline in Configuration K in the latter period of the study of 1.3 percent. As the average devoted to Configuration K over the entire fourteen-year period is 21.4 percent, more than one-fifth of the two accounting journals combined is concerned with accounting's role in protecting the public, a percentage that remains fairly consistent over the period. Why is this configuration consistently emphasized as a view of society and accounting in the profession's literature? How does Configuration K present the profession's role in a manner that conforms to different economic and social circumstances?

One interpretation is that Configuration K presents a role for accounting that appeals to society, i.e., legitimizes the profession, under a variety of social and economic circumstances. For example, consider the image of an accountant that is alluded to: an ethical, incorruptible, and fair professional who is dedicated to serving the needs of third-party users—those who do not have access to this information other than to relying upon the reports that management prepares. The independent accountants, by auditing these statements, ensure the adequacy and fairness of these reports. This benevolent, civil, and wholesome image of the profession is an expedient strategy used to promote the profession over a variety of economic and social circumstances.

In Discourse Category #34, the integrity and expertise of accountants are described as attributes making accountants natural candidates for developing public policies. Accountants are well-suited for assisting in local community decisions (such as school board proposals), and on higher levels, assisting the state in its budgeting process, and improving Defense Department accounting procedures. Articles disclose the harmonious and contributory manner in which the profession has assisted in protecting society's interests: in cracking down on crime, in budgeting for national objectives, in restoring public confidence in the tax system because of the use of certified public accountants, and in ensuring national security through accounting's input in defense matters. One editorial states "the public interest is involved in everything the CPA does" (*Journal of Accountancy*, November 1971). These articles suggest that students and others should be more aware of the dynamic nature of the accountant and the accountant's responsibility in achieving public goals. The contribution of the accountant as a public policy assistant, or statesperson is a discursive strategy which might be desirable across varying circumstances.

Articles in Discursive Category #36 suggest the profession should aggressively promote its own self-interests because the interests of the profession are compatible with and enhance society's interests. For example, articles insist that the profession should not allow competitive bidding on audits because this would jeopardize the ethical conduct of accountants and their clients. In order to reduce fees, quality and high standards might be traded off, which is clearly not in the interest of the public. The articles insist that restrictions on advertising and solicitation appear to be in the self-interest of accountants, but their sole purpose is to ensure quality audits and to protect the public interest.

Notably, these positions regarding advertising and competition came under scrutiny by the Federal Trade Commission, the Justice Department, and the Securities and Exchange

Commission in the 1980s, when policies to deregulate industry and commerce were installed with a vengeance in the Reagan-Thatcher era. For the accounting profession, the discursive realm that prohibiting advertising was "in the public interest" collided with the need for autonomy and self-regulation: it was the state that argued bans on solicitation and advertising and restrictions on commissions and contingent fees were not in the public interest. The accounting profession, under pressure and with much internal debate, agreed to eliminate some of these restrictions in pronouncements of the AICPA Code of Ethics in 1978 and 1988. Seen as an act of preserving self-regulation, and as a compromise with the state, the rhetoric that these practices are not necessarily in the public interest continued to be murmured by many practitioners.

Comparison of the Accounting Journals: Configuration K

Although the above indicates little variance in the results for Configuration K, there are significant differences between the journals. Throughout the period of study the *Journal of Accountancy* devotes a far greater proportion to Configuration K discourses. This applies as an average over all years, and for different periodizations as well.

For the fourteen years of the study, the *Journal of Accountancy* devotes 30 percent of its editorials to these discourses, while the *Accounting Review*'s percentage is substantially less, an average of 12.8 percent. The difference between the journals is most striking in the latter portion of our study. During the 1970 through 1973 period, Configuration K accounted for 33.5 percent of the articles published by the *Journal of Accountancy,* which is more than four times the average of 7 percent demonstrated by the *Accounting Review* for the same years. See Figure 4.

The *Journal of Accountancy* consistently devotes approximately one-third of its pages to discourses characteristic of Configuration K. Promoting the accounting profession's responsibility to the public can be interpreted as another example of the public relations realm of the *Journal of Accountancy*. As the official commentator of the American Institute of Certified Public Accountants, the *Journal of Accountancy* is committed to advocating a reputable, conscientious, and untarnished image of the profession.

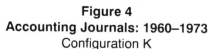

Figure 4
Accounting Journals: 1960–1973
Configuration K

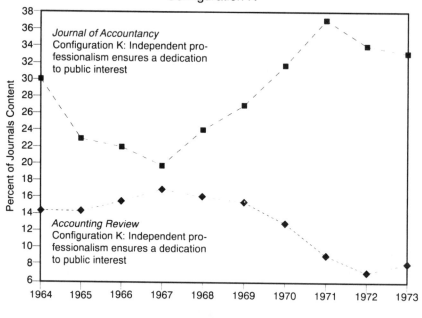

Why would the early Seventies be a period when the accounting profession would continue to promote the public interest view of society of Configuration K? One explanation is that this discursive realm replaces other discourses that have failed to form social cohesion, and are now rendered ineffective. Recall that during the early Seventies there is a decline in the *Journal of Accountancy*'s concentration in Configuration J, celebrating the profession's contribution to business profit and economic growth. During the Seventies' era of falling rates or profits, it becomes incongruous for the professional journal to glorify harmony in the marketplace and the profession's success in generating profit. As an alternative, the benefits of accounting are increasingly manifested in Configuration K's advocacy of the ethical, principled, and just accountant.

Relatedly, claiming that the profession is devoted to serving the public may also be a part of the *Journal of Accountancy*'s defense for the profession against its critics in the early Seventies, including congressional investigations of the adequacy of audits in preventing manipulation and fraud (e.g., the Moss and Metcalf investigations). These deliberations questioned the profession's inadequate standards for maintaining independence, and whether the profession was serving its public mandate. These charges resulted in a dismantling of much of the rule-making apparatus that was under attack (the Accounting Principles Board) and a commitment to improved standard setting through a new assembly, the Financial Accounting Standards Board.

The *Journal of Accountancy*'s increase in Configuration K might also be a way of attracting recruits, consistent with its status as a professional journal. During the early Seventies there was a shortage of professional recruits; claiming that accountants are dynamic statespeople involved in public policies may entice entrants into the field.

Unlike the results for the *Journal of Accountancy*, the percentage that the *Accounting Review* devotes to Configuration K decreases in the latter period of the study. From an average of 15.1 percent in the 1960–1969 period, the *Accounting Review*'s average drops 8.1 percent, in the 1970–1973 period, to an average of 7 percent. The *Accounting Review* appears to be, overall, much less concerned with the ethical and independent character of accountants or the public role of accountants assisting in state policies, i.e., less concerned with the characteristics of a practicing accountant. The usefulness of accounting is promoted by the *Accounting Review* in terms of other attributes, for example, its contribution to the efficient allocation of resources, and the promotion of statistical techniques (Configurations J and L, respectively).

The results would support the conceptualization of the *Accounting Review* as technique-oriented (Briloff, 1990; Okcabol, 1989; Tinker, 1985; Williams, 1985; Zeff, 1978, 1983). This technical orientation increases as the *Accounting Review* increasingly trades off articles concerning ethics and public policies, and promotes, instead, methods of measurement in the 1970–1973 period. In the 1970–1973 period the *Accounting Review* devotes only 7 percent of its literature to discourse categories in Configuration K, in contrast to the *Journal of Accountancy*'s intensity of concentration in Configuration K, 33.5 percent, during the same period.

Accounting Configuration L

The two discourse categories comprising Configuration L encourage the use of computers and statistical techniques for a variety of purposes. For example, articles state that the use of statistical analysis assists investors and financial advisers in financial statement analysis, aids managers in their profit goals, and can be useful in academic research. A common theme in Configuration L is the claim that accountants have a natural role to play in the development of statistical techniques and computerized systems (i.e., electronic data processing [EDP]). This is due to accountants' expertise in broad areas of business, especially information systems. As accountants are trained in areas that are needed to develop and construct these techniques, the profession is portrayed as an integral part of innovations and further use of these techniques.

Table XV
Accounting Configuration L:
Advocating the use of statistical techniques, and the expertise of accountants in developing computerized information systems.

Percentages Devoted to Configuration L:

1960/61–1966/67	9.7%
1967/68–1973/74	9.5%
Decrease	0.2%

Discourses in this configuration include:

♦ Statistical techniques are advanced for a range of applications in auditing and accounting research;

♦ Praise for accountants' expertise and natural role in developing computerized information systems.

Note: The presentation of dual years reflects a one year lag for the *Accounting Review*.

The empirical results indicate little variation in the percentages devoted to Configuration L. The decreases are minor. The percentage for this configuration is 9.5 percent for the entire period of study, 1960 through 1973. The results illustrate that the profession consistently promotes its abilities with business statistics and computerized information systems, which coincides with the (broad) increasing use of these technologies in the 1960 through 1973 period. What are the characteristics of Configuration L that advance a role or an image of the profession that would explain the consistent emphasis?

During the 1960 through 1973 period, the increases in new technologies placed a burden on the profession to explore these areas as well in order to maintain clients and to demonstrate the profession's usefulness and relevance. Articles in Configuration L describe accounting as a fundamental component of information systems and electronic data processing, thereby making accountants proficient in these areas. The articles claim that outsiders (non-accountants) recognize the expertise of accountants and support a broad role for accountants in developing information systems. Articles in Configuration L encourage accountants to develop computer applications for expanding audit controls and internal organizational controls—additional areas in which accountants are proficient. The importance of educating accounting students and recruits in statistical techniques and computerized information systems is another common emphasis of articles in Configuration L. Training in these areas is viewed as an important responsibility of the profession and educational goals should reflect and encourage accounting's role in computer developments.

In Discourse Category #37, articles characterize statistical information as imbued with special properties. Thus, statistical data are regarded as superior to the prior information used by accountants, auditors, and management in the decision-making process (i.e., statistics develop an omnipotence). Statistical information is promoted for its objectivity and quality of definition and thus provides more accurate results (e.g., in determining depreciation and net income). Articles advance the objectivity in which the technique, statistics, is applied to the social phenomenon, business performance. Articles frequently claim that the use of advanced statistical methods automatically benefits financial statement users and society. However, the concentration on methodology in measuring business performance does not imply a natural benefit to users and society if the measure (e.g., net income) is not suitable for the users. A characteristic of articles in Configuration L is that there is no reflection on the object of measure; questions are not raised as to the meaning of the ultimate measure.

Quantification of decision-making processes (e.g. lease evaluations under uncertainty) are described in these articles as the type of information that accountants are particularly suited to provide and should not be left to other professionals. Articles in Configuration L view accountants as having an important role to play in the sharpening of the decisional process.

Comparison of the Accounting Journals: Configuration L

When the two journals are analyzed separately, the results are quite different. One difference is particularly striking, that the editorials in the *Journal of Accountancy* do not discuss the use of statistical and quantitative methods. The score of Discourse Category #37, concerned with statistics, is zero percent for the *Journal of Accountancy* throughout the period. The *Journal of Accountancy* does, however, discuss in its editorials computerized information systems. This would be coded in Discourse Category #38, a category devoted to computer technology and data processing as information systems, with little concern for statistics or quantitative techniques. Although the editorials do not advance the use of statistics, the *Journal of Accountancy* is concerned with the role of accounting in computerized information systems.

One interpretation of these results for the *Journal of Accountancy* is that they conform with a view of the *Journal of Accountancy* as a practitioner-oriented publication. During the 1960s the *Journal of Accountancy* supported practitioners for their knowledge and natural involvement in computer applications. In some cases, the editorials are concerned and apprehensive that if practitioners do not accept responsibility for increasing their knowledge in electronic data processing, other professionals, such as specialists in management information systems, will fill the gap that accountants are creating. Alternatively, the editorials state, the profession should look upon the computerization of information systems as a new opportunity for practitioners to demonstrate their importance and ability to assist in these developing technologies. Concerned with competition from other professions, the journal calls upon practitioners to advance the image of the profession and increase the services that practitioners offer their clients.

For the entire period 1960–1973, and for both periodization analyses, the *Accounting Review* consistently devotes a greater percentage to Configuration L than the *Journal of Accountancy*. The *Accounting Review* devotes an average of 14.9 percent to Configuration L for the fourteen years of the study in contrast to the *Journal of Accountancy*'s average of 4.1 percent for the entire 1960–1973 period, a 10.8 percent difference. However, the difference between the two journals is substantially the result of Discourse Category #37, concerning statistical methods, and is not attributable to Discourse Category #38, which is concerned with computerized information systems.

For the 1960–1973 period, the *Accounting Review* devotes 9.8 percent of its articles to the application of statistics, Category #37, versus zero percent for the *Journal of Accountancy* for the entire period of the study. Articles in the *Accounting Review* frequently justify the use of statistics in academic research because other disciplines have used these techniques.

The increasing use of advanced statistical techniques in academic journals has been regarded as a problem because it limits the opportunity for exploring larger questions and concentrates on puzzle solving instead. (This has been argued in previous sections, e.g., Briloff, 1990; Tinker, 1985; Williams, 1985; Zeff, 1978, 1983). Mautz (1974) laments, "For goodness sake, what has happened to the *Accounting Review*? Most of us, and here I include academic types as well as practitioners, find this foreign language material almost impossible to read . . . an illustration of how far apart academic and applied accounting have become" (p. 356). The results here indicate that the *Accounting Review*'s concentration on statistical methods increases, with its discourse on statistics averaging 17 percent during the 1970 1973 period. This raises the concern as to whether the technique orientation of academic research can be restrained in order to provide opportunities for exploring different research questions.

Accounting Configuration M

Configuration M combines articles concerned with international relationships, such as American military involvement overseas, the accounting practices of multinationals, and the accounting organizations that are responsible for resolving international disputes. Articles in this configuration praise America's commitment to a strong defense and economy because it ensures international freedom (e.g., against communism during the cold war years) and promotes democracy.

In this configuration, accounting's role in global freedom is viewed as crucial. It is claimed that accounting, because it

---

Table XVI
Accounting Configuration M:
Promoting the international benefits of accounting; praising its contribution to economic and social freedom, international trade and competition, and global democracy.

Percentages Devoted to Configuration M:

1960/61–1966/67	5.6%
1967/68–1973/74	0.8%
Decrease	4.8%

Discourses in this configuration include:
♦ Advancing international freedom and democracy;
♦ Praising U.S.'s competition in international markets, and accounting's contribution to U.S. success;
♦ Accounting's contribution to the global benefits of market capitalism and growth.

Note: The presentation of dual years reflects a one year lag for the *Accounting Review*.

---

provides economic information and information on defense spending, assists in the decisions that governments must make in order to defend democracies against communism. Thus, these articles contend, accounting assists in defending world freedom.

Another characteristic of articles in Configuration M is their praise for accounting's contribution to U.S. success in international competition. For example, accounting's role in promoting uniformity in international standards of reporting, and the profession's policy of non-restriction of accounting practice abroad, are credited as beneficial to American business. Articles in Configuration M argue that accounting contributes to global economic and social well-being because accounting aids in the free flow of capital between countries. In this configuration, market capitalism and economic growth are viewed as universally beneficial, in a global sense, and it is claimed that accounting is a beneficial component of capitalism's overall benevolence.

As the above summary data in Table XVI indicate, this configuration does not receive, in comparison to the other configurations, a substantial percentage in the accounting literature. For the entire period of study, the average for Configuration M is 3.1 percent. During the earlier years of the study, 1960 through 1966, the average percentage is 5.6 percent; this declines to only .8 percent, a decrease of 4.8 percent during 1967–1973 (almost an elimination of Configuration M). The results for the accounting literature differ from the findings for *Fortune* magazine's related Configuration E, which concentrated on "championing U.S. interests, values and business practices in international affairs." On average over the 1960–1973 period, *Fortune* magazine devoted 13 percent of its feature articles to this configuration. During the same period, however, the accounting literature devotes only 3.2 percent to specifying accounting's role in international affairs. The view of society that the profession concentrates on is more frequently limited to non-international roles of accounting, although accounting clearly does have a role in international affairs.

Comparison of the Accounting Journals: Configuration M

Overall, the *Journal of Accountancy* concentrates on Configuration M to a greater extent than the *Accounting Review* does; an average of 4.9 percent compared to 1.4 percent, respectively, for the entire fourteen-year period. The difference between the journals is greatest during the early part of the study; in the 1960–1966 period the *Journal of Accountancy* devotes 8.4 percent to Configuration M. In contrast, the percentage is 2.7 percent for the *Accounting Review*. For both journals, 1960 through 1966 is a period when the proportion devoted to Configuration M is highest. The *Journal of Accountancy*'s percentage declines 6.9 percent, from the 8.4 percent average in 1960–1966, to only 1.5 percent in the 1967–1973 period; the *Accounting Review*'s percentage declines to zero percent in the 1967–1973 period.

Neither accounting journal concentrates on an international perspective of accounting; however, the *Journal of Accountancy*'s editorials did present these issues in the earlier years. During the cold war years of the early 1960s, the *Journal of Accountancy* editorials claim that the United States is a protector of global freedom and has a responsibility to support economic growth (and thus social well-being) in underdeveloped countries. The editorials insist that economic strength in these countries ensures well-being and dignity for their people. Articles contended that new nations were in desperate need of capital funds, and "if they cannot attract investments from abroad, their only apparent alternative is the communist method of squeezing capital out of their own people by depressing the standard of living even below the present level" (*Journal of Accountancy*, January 1961, p. 35). The editorials argue that accounting, because it provides a reliable means of reporting how capital is used, encourages foreign investments and contributes to economic development of the underdeveloped countries. The editorial laments, "Too few political leaders, either abroad or in the United States, seem to understand the importance of international accounting to the growth of trade and investment in the free world" (ibid.).

Why do discourses on international roles of accounting decrease in the latter period of the study? One possible explanation is that the profession was preoccupied with solving more immediate pressures. During the latter years of the study, there was increasing criticism of the profession by Congress. The empirical results confirm that discourse categories were concerned with the internal organization of the profession and conflicts with the state that increased during this period. Another interpretation is that part of the increasing critique against the profession was related to international misconduct of corporations. The Foreign Corrupt Practices Act (1977) was partly the result of a lack of confidence in the accounting profession's concern or ability to uncover illegal acts of U.S. corporations abroad. The *Journal of Accountancy* may have deemed it imprudent to promote accounting's involvement in international affairs during the early Seventies.

The *Journal of Accountancy*'s editorials, as is illustrated above, embraced rhetoric on the role of accounting in the free world, to a limited extent, in the early Sixties. However, the *Accounting Review*'s concentration is even more limited than the *Journal of Accountancy*. Articles appearing in the *Accounting Review* do not indicate a reflection on accounting's international role in promoting freedom, or preventing communism or whether encouraging foreign investments is benevolent or exploitative to the host countries. These may be the research questions that have been traded off by the *Accounting Review*, concentrating instead on discourses concerning measurement techniques and the efficient allocation of resources (Discourse Categories #37 and #31, respectively).

Accounting Configuration N: Sundry Discourses

Included in this section are discourses that appear in the two accounting journals infrequently and were not combined with any of the previous configurations. As these miscellaneous categories averaged between 3 and 4 percent through the period, with little change, no summary results are reported in a separate table. One of the categories receiving limited presentation was a combination of articles advocating the interests of the accounting profession without rationalizing that this objective was beneficial to society's interest (which would be coded in Configuration K). Included in this miscellaneous configuration are articles debating corporate social responsibility issues, viewed from the perspective that these concerns are a part of larger problems in society. These and other issues were sporadic, illustrating that discourses which are ignored can be as significant as those that are emphasized, issues we address below.

Marginalized Accounting Discourses and Accounting's Social Role

Social accounting and corporate social responsibility accounting emerged during the early period of study, lagging the larger social responsibility and social welfare movement of the 1960s. Social accounting was considered a reform movement, responding to the growing criticisms of corporations regarding environmental and racial rights issues and concern for employee safety and consumer protection, while remaining faithful to conventional accounting and its neo-classical affiliations. Accounting researchers argued for the recognition of externalities in financial statements—costs and benefits incurred by parties not responsible for the action leading to these consequences—in order to monitor the social impact of corporate behavior.

The discourse of social accounting separated these social concerns from the realm of accounting proper, intended to separate the notion of social and behavioral aspects from economic realms. Rather than conceive of all of accounting as embedded with conflict between social groups, social accounting implies that there exists an accounting proper that is not concerned with the full range of corporate activities, and a separate category of accounting that takes corporate accountability into consideration. This two-tier separation represses and excludes from the mainstream of accounting the centrality of corporate consequences on all social realms (employees' job-related injuries and illnesses, pollution and environmental degradation, racial and sex discrimination, bribes to foreign countries, etc.). If accounting proper embraced all social interests, then this two-tier classification, and the need for a separate social audit, would be unnecessary. By distinguishing between social accounting and the realm of accounting proper, certain interests are disenfranchised and denied, while those of others are privileged and granted legitimacy and power.

Implicit in these distinctions between social accounting and accounting proper is the view that private interests are different and separable from public interests. Yet all interests are private insofar as they refer to a subset of social members, and all interests are public or social in that they refer to rights, duties, responsibilities, and obligations that are endowed on social members by virtue of their interrelated roles under particular social structures (be it feudalism or capitalism). By accounting for only private enterprise, accountants claim an erroneous neutrality and impartiality in the public domain.

Noticeably absent from the discursive practices in the 1960–1973 period was the call for ethics that was so prevalent in the 1980s and early 1990s. Previously considered a private moral matter, the changing landscape of business suggests that a lack of an ethical concern for the social interest contributes to the corruption and greed flourishing in the merger mania years of the 1980s. The lack of ethical discussion in the *Accounting Review* is particularly striking, as academics are expected to foster the climate of a discipline. By denying any moral or social responsibility, researchers have been accused of contributing to the demise in morals and proliferating a creed of technicians ill-equipped to reckon with the broad implications of business activity. The profession's research and practitioner journals play a role in creating and representing the accounting world. By denying that ethics and moral concerns (over a wide range of social issues) is of fundamental importance, and by granting profit maximization a primary and privileged status, the profession elects economic efficiency over ethics.

It is not the case that educators and the literature do not teach or emulate an ethical position—that they are somehow able to remain neutral. Indeed there is pontification of an ethic and a promotion of an ethical and moral stance in the literature—one of promoting social Darwinism, competition rather than cooperation, and the sacrosanct status of efficiency and profit—at any cost to others. Cultivation of critical thinking and advancing inquiry into the numerous constituencies affected by accounting's adjudication is excluded from accounting literature and education. Neglecting these conflicts produces many of the contemporary financial failures, lawsuits, bankruptcies, bailouts, and related unemployment increases, and cuts in social programs.

In contrast to the dearth of moral and ethical references in the 1960–1973 literature, the 1980s have witnessed a clarion call to include an ethics course in accounting and business curriculums and to foster and train employees on ethics—with numerous companies publishing guides, brochures, and policy statements on the ethical position and desired ethical climate of the firm. An institutional call for ethics does not contradict the contention that social concerns are ignored. The recent increase in promoting ethics serves to constrain the system and ensure its survival. Ethical behavior is an informal control of disciplining an otherwise untamed marketplace in which all participants have been affected by the negative consequences of unconstrained greed and competition. Scandals in investment banking and the securities market and greenmail are costly to all firms and their managers. These events generate a loss in confidence in management's stewardship ability and in the system in general. They result in precarious capital and debt structures causing volatility in interest rates and the uncertainty and fear regarding takeovers undermines the productivity of employees and management. At some point the effect of individualism and competition becomes overwhelmingly detrimental rather than purposeful to the functioning of the system and jeopardizes the survival of major participants in it. This situation necessitates implementation of regulation and other forms of control, including the ideological realm of appealing to ethics.

Our advocacy of ethics should not be misconstrued that morals and ethics are desirable because they ensure survival of the system. Nor are we concerned that the problematic consequences of unethical behavior are detriments to business. Rather, we wish to highlight the broad deleterious effects on the environment, the sacrifices of human life, and the suffering of employees as the outcomes of corporate behavior that ignore these issues (e.g., Hooker Chemical's waste disposal in Love Canal, Nestle's international promotion of powdered milk, and Manville's employees' use of asbestos).

The current discourse to "harbor in a new ethics" in accounting and business shares some of the rhetorical dimensions of social accounting literature. Ethics, like social accounting, is seen as a separate issue, dichotomized from the socio-political issues of the day and failing to include not only business costs, but the broader social sacrifices of corporate decisions. Accountants are implicated in social issues when setting disclosure rules for the restructuring of international debts, when formulating standards for funding pension plans, and when they contend that pollution costs should be excluded from financial statements because they defy measurement. Yet the literature denies the public effect of day-to-day practices of accounting and that it inevitably takes sides in social policy.

Notes

1. The review of business and accounting literature is confined to the United States.

2. An analysis was conducted to determine the relationship between *Journal of Accountancy* editorials and feature articles. Frequently, the editorials are a lead-in to an issue discussed as a main article, news report, or regular column. Summary results of the analysis indicate the following (these are averaged for the fourteen-year period):

   34% of the editorials related to a feature article
   43% of the editorials related to a news report, statement in quote, etc. (not a feature article)
   23% of the editorials did not relate to other columns
   100% Total

3. *Fortune*'s computations concerning the representation of the Fortune 500 group indicates the 500's share of the industrial economy rose over the years. Their share of total industrial sales rose from around one-half in 1954 to approximately two-thirds in 1974. Their share of earnings rose from two-thirds to three-quarters over the same two decades. *Fortune* comments on the concentration that has occurred: "There is no doubt, then, that the 500 largest industrials are a substantially greater chunk of the U.S. economy than they were when *Fortune* began compiling these lists" (May 1975, p. 240).

4. The notion of statistical significance and variation when interpreting the results of a study is a relative notion (e.g., the universe or population is rarely studied; a sample is studied instead). In this study, *Fortune* and the accounting journals are regarded as instruments for affecting and reflecting social disputes; as journals commanding widespread popularity and support, they constitute substantial samples of the discursive population. Therefore, a change in the percentages for *Fortune*'s discourse categories or configurations (or for the *Journal of Accountancy* or the *Accounting Review*) are considered important in and of themselves.

CHAPTER VI

SIGNS AND SYMBOLS: REDISCOVERING ACCOUNTING'S PARTISANSHIP

This book's aim—to explore the roles of accounting in society—takes its point of departure from the orthodoxy in its focus on social conflict. It disputes claims that accountancy can be neutral in conflicts over the distribution of wealth in society, and rejects the image of accounting as an impartial mediator merely representing and recording the facts. This claim is refuted epistemologically, socially, and historically.

We began our assessment of accounting's role by observing the controversies plaguing the profession; the examples were only a selection of the many battlefields in which accounting is a contested terrain. The reliance on accounting numbers, and the lawsuits that have recently soared for the profession's potential liability to outside users, have led to a crisis in the "expectations gap" and a revision of the auditor's most treasured and preserved document—the auditor opinion statement. The Auditing Standards Board (ASB) released in 1988 what has become known as the expectation gap SASs (Statement on Auditing Standards Nos. 53-61) in an effort to reduce the discrepancy between what the public construes as an auditor's responsibility and what auditors regard as their accountability. The debate particularly relates to the auditor's role in detecting and disclosing errors, irregularities, and illegal acts of clients. In contrast to the stated goal of reducing the gap, scholars in the American

Bar Association have concluded that the SASs are ill-conceived, confusing, debasing to the profession, and unrealistically enlarge the public's expectations, potentially making the accounting profession a scapegoat for mishaps.

Such events demonstrate the public arena in which the profession participates as a protagonist, clearly unable to avoid the role of adjudicator. The expectations gap reveals the wide umbrella under which the profession participates in social choices; the early references to savings and loans failures and merger mania illustrate the profession's involvement more specifically. Congressional judgement and the legal profession's response regarding the SASs' objectives indicates accounting misconceives its relationship with financial statement users, and the reckoning necessary to serve the public.

The profession's responsibility extends not only to immediate financial statement users, but to others affected by classification schemes and disclosure rules. Congress has recently recognized the controversial nature of pension plans, and the accounting treatment for disclosing liability has been the subject of intense debate. Over the past decade thousands of companies have withdrawn over $20 billion from overfunded pension plans, provoking a controversy in Congress as to who has the right to the overfunded amounts (*Wall Street Journal*, February 12, 1990). A pension counsel for the House Labor Management Relations Subcommittee observed, "The money was put aside for retirement. It is really deferred compensation. It's not the company's" (*The New York Times*, February 1, 1987). As pension plans affect over 53 million Americans, a number of issues are expected to be examined by Congress, including the right of workers who change jobs and how to ensure the financial viability of the Pension Benefit Guarantee Corporation, which insures pension workers whose companies default on their obligations.

Controversies escalated recently as more firms terminated their pension funds when high interest rates and a rising stock market helped many retirement plans reap unusually high returns. Corporations skimmed off pension surpluses to reduce debt, to finance capital investment, and to make acquisitions. Companies do this by closing the funds, referred to as terminating the plan, using part of the money to buy securities to cover future retirement obligations, and keeping the difference. New securities are not always of the caliber of the original plan, and some employees' funds are invested in high risk junk bonds. Curbs on junk investments by savings and loans institutions are part of the thrift industry bailout bill passed by Congress, and a similar caution applicable to pension plans is being considered (*Wall Street Journal*, February 12, 1990).

The importance of ensuring the financial viability of the Pension Benefits Guarantee Corporation (PBGC) and to guard against unscrupulous use of the PBGC's assets has been recognized in a crucial victory for the PBGC in the Supreme Court. The court ruled that the federal agency has the power to make an employer take back responsibility for pension obligations, and resume liabilities for pension plans previously terminated. The case emerged out of a suit by the agency against LTV Corporation, which had been allowed to stop funding three underfunded plans shortly after the firm filed for bankruptcy in 1986. The PBGC assumed the pension plan liabilities for $2.1 billion, the portion insured by the federal agency. Yet a few months later, under pressure from the United Steelworkers of America, LTV instituted a program to provide benefits similar to those in the terminated plan. The court ruling confers the agency's assertion that the new plan was an abuse of federal pension law and an attempt to transfer liability from LTV to the federal agency. "All retirees can feel more secure because the Supreme Court has upheld PBGC's authority to protect the insurance program against abuse," stated James B. Lockhart, executive director of the PBGC (*The New York Times*, June 19, 1990).

The Supreme Court ruling demonstrates that corporations will be liable for terminating a pension plan if the employees have been inadequately compensated. In a termination of a pension plan employees typically receive annuities in lieu of their future pension benefits. U. S. Senator Howard Metzenbaum has estimated that these annuities are often worth as little as forty-five cents for every dollar of original pension benefit. The Supreme Court's intervention recognizes that the pension plan has an implicit contract with employees (for cost of living and promotion adjustments) amounting to a sizable proportion of the remaining fifty-five cents.

Accountants and actuaries determine what is needed to assure workers' pensions. The question as to what firms are liable for ranges from the explicit written minimum, activated by the rare event of a termination, or the larger amount, implied by the going concern concept of the firm and its related long-term relationship with employees. In other post-retirement debates the courts have concluded that enforceability depends not only on legal documents, but on oral and written communications to employees and the past practices of the company (Ghicas and Tinker, 1990). Accounting practices choose to undervalue pension liabilities by using the minimum liquidation value for liabilities, corresponding to the value of an insurance annuity to discharge the pension obligation at the moment of termination. Yet this amount is typically less than the going concern value, as it makes no provision for future vesting, promotion, cost of living, and other increases expected in the employee's relation to the firm. The denial of these social costs illustrates accounting choice in pension conflicts, and by taking sides with firms to account for and disclose only the minimum obligation, it is understandable that employees and labor unions will contest the treatment. The Supreme Court's ruling illustrates that taking account for pension obligations is not a neutral practice, but a distributional one.

Crafting Accounting

Rejecting the notion that classification decisions can be neutral, the noted Harvard paleontologist Stephen J. Gould questions the "science" that classifies some highly addictive lethal drugs as legal (such as alcohol and tobacco) while declaring criminal other more innocuous substances (such as marijuana) (Moore, 1991). Gould dismisses the objectivist pretensions of all naming, writing that :

> Taxonomy, or the study of classification, occupies a low status among the sciences because most people view the activity as a kind of glorified bookkeeping dedicated to pasting objects into preassigned spaces in nature's stamp album. This mistaken judgment rests on the false premise that our categories are given by nature and ascertained by simple, direct observation. . . . [O]ur classifications are human impositions, or at least culturally based decisions on what to stress among a plethora of viable alternatives (Gould, 1990, p. 73).

This implies that there are no positively or empirically identified "drugs"—or "firms" or "costs" or "profits" for that matter;

there are only human definitions and interventions as to what these terms mean (Moore, 1991).

The analysis of accounting and business literature provided here is a means of examining accounting's choice of classification, and thus its role in the mediation of social conflicts. The results of the discourse study confirms that the accounting literature emphasizes different roles of accounting during different periods, illustrating that the profession's roles are not immutable; rather, they modify and change, and can be transformed and altered. In this manner the discourse categories evident in accounting literature help create, perpetuate, and constitute a social ideology that obscures, naturalizes, and transforms social conflict.

A summary of the main discourses in the accounting literature during the period of study, 1960 through 1973, is presented in Table XI. The promotion of accounting's contribution to society as a well-organized, regulatory mechanism that is superior to the state is captured by Configuration H (35.1 percent for the study period). The accounting contribution to the efficient allocation of social resources is reflected in Configuration J (27.1 percent). The role of accounting as a public protector serving the public interest (Configuration K) averages 21.4 percent over the study period. Configuration L emphasizes the use of statistical techniques and computer applications (9.5 percent). Accounting's role in international issues (Configuration M) averages 3.1 percent. We saw that the *Journal of Accountancy* and the *Accounting Review* contribute to these discourses quite differently in different periods.

Controversy between the accounting profession and state regulators, managers, stockholders, pension investors, homeowners, thrift depositors, insurance policy holders, employees, and numerous other constituencies are ultimately conflicts over the distribution of income and wealth. The academic literature's failure to acknowledge the profession's participation in social conflict leaves the latter ill-prepared to respond to critiques, challenges, and attacks by various social constituencies.

The unstable position of accounting, arising from its involvement in conflict over the distribution of income, is evidenced by a whole series of recent disputes: conflicts over accounting's cost-based pricing for utilities; the provision for employee pensions through the accounting expense; financial disclosures by banks of their overseas loans; the pricing of armaments purchased by the military from General Dynamics and other contractors; and the accountability of corporate management (failure by accounting in this realm has opened the door to speculators, green-mailers, and other "corrective" mechanisms). Each of these cases highlights the inadequacy of a representational view of accounting, whether it be the price determination of armaments or utility rates or the inadequacy of pension provisions. Accounting does not merely reflect the reality of conflict, it determines and shapes it.

The above examples raised doubts about the self-declared role of the profession in society. The impartiality of accounting is challenged by the results of this study—accounting policies and theories are disputed because they are powerful tools in advancing (and obscuring) the interests that accounting serves. These are continuous disputes because in capitalist society conflicts over the distribution of wealth are endemic and ubiquitous.

The literature study offers special insight into changes in the states' management of social conflict. The period of study, 1960 through 1973, was characterized as a period of crises, in which the very mechanisms for mediating and resolving conflict were transformed. The results of the study illustrate various changes that are summarized as a movement from "management by consent" to "management by coercion." Although a precise dating of this hegemonic shift is not possible, the literature review suggests that it occurred in the late 1960s.

The study illustrates that during the period, support of the state's role as a manager of conflict through mediation changed once the state adopted a more authoritarian stand. This is evidenced by the increase in discourses criticizing the state (Configuration B). The movements of the other discourses also imply a more favorable climate for rule by authority rather than by consent. This is illustrated in the decrease of *Fortune* discourses directed at organizational harmony (Configuration C) and the increase in discourses welcoming control by an impersonal competitive environment, ruled by the ethic of the survival of the fittest (Configuration D). The accounting literature joins *Fortune* in its criticism of the state, and warrants the accounting role as the optimal social regulator (Configuration H). As the economic crises intensify, discourses promoting the benevolence of the marketplace decline; and there is a decrease in discourses advocating the role of accounting in eliciting consent (Configurations J and K, respectively).

The differences between the two accounting journals is sometimes striking. The *Journal of Accountancy* serves as a public relations forum, advocating the profession's contribution to society as an industrial statesperson and as a public servant that strictly adheres to a code of ethics to ensure that the public's best interests are served. The *Journal of Accountancy* deliberates on controversies with government and professional organizations to a greater extent than the *Accounting Review*. The latter journal increasingly emphasizes asocial and apolitical questions about the need for a proper income measure and asset valuation. Discourses which are de-emphasized by the *Accounting Review* during the later (authoritarian) period of the study are those promoting ethics and public interest objectives. The *Accounting Review's* concentration on objective measures and the efficient allocation of resources reflects this trade-off with other issues. Yet research reveals in rewriting the history of accounting that:

> one can subvert the belief that accounting develops functionally as a passive tool of economic efficiency. Instead, the history of accounting is interpreted as a complex web of economic, political and accidental co-occurrences that mirror neither technical rationality nor a necessary progress (Arrington and Frances, 1989a, p. 2).

Accounting's privileged access to key decisional areas in economic and civil society immerses the profession in controversial disputes; accountants' involvement inevitably advance the interests of certain groups in these disputes. Yet, accounting theorists continue to claim that accountants are impartial, and disinterested recorders of fact—this obscures and distorts the role that accounting plays in social conflict. As long as the academic community bars the systematic study of social conflict from its apparatus, it will continue to offer one-sided partisan prescriptions, and invite the wrath of those who are victims of its partisanship. Alternatively, given that accounting researchers must take sides in social disputes, an inquiry into accounting's partisanship could be an exploration into roles of the profession that are more worthy for society.

Examples of re-examination of a discipline's social constitution have emerged in the legal profession, with feminist theorists providing redefinitions. Scholars have exposed the male emphasis on rights and abstractions embodied in the legal definition of contract, the doctrine of negligence, and rape, and propose a radical and feminine redefinition of what is an injury and what is a crime. These efforts seek to show that legal principles are not uncontroversial but in fact inevitably and historically contingent, gender and race-biased, ideologically loaded, and operate in a way to preserve the dominance of those who codify them. Similarly, the excluded and dominated voices in an accounting discipline must be exposed to serious policy debate to transform its repressive nature.

The recent major transformations in the political climate in Eastern Europe and the former Soviet Union suggest an era of social and economic changes of historical significance. As these countries consider shifts toward increased private enterprises, a reduction in state operation of industry, and the implementation of market economies, the experience of the West is looked upon as a prototype for establishing new economic systems in the East. In the past, the role of accounting—to report on state-owned enterprises—served a very different set of purposes from that in Western economies, and accounting's new import is being recognized and fostered. "Perhaps it won't be an exaggeration to say that the accounting philosophy can be a new, common language of the future of the international community" stated Lajos Faluvegi, President-elect of the European Accounting Association (EAA) at its Annual Congress in Budapest in 1990. Emphasizing the crucial new significance of accounting in the transformation of the economic system, he stated in addressing the congress that "without an accounting system there can be no market economy."

As accounting's role expands in these global contexts, and as Western notions of accountability are transferred to other countries, we are cautious that the subject base itself as a responsive and publicly accountable discipline. In situating accounting as a subject with public responsibility, we are not redefining accountancy—adjudicating exchanges has always been the subject's social function. What we propose is restoring this social function to pride of place in the accounting research agenda, together with the conflicts and allegiances it entails.

BIBLIOGRAPHY

Adorno, Theodor. *Negative Dialectics*. Translated by B. Ashton. New York: Seabury Press, 1973.

Allen, V. L. *Social Analysis: A Marxist Critique and Alternative*. London: Longman, 1975.

Althusser, Louis and Balibar, Etienne. *Reading Capital*. London: New Left Books, 1970.

Althusser, Louis. "Ideology and Ideological State Apparatus." In *Lenin and Philosophy and Other Essays*. London: Allen Lane, 1971.

_____. *Essays in Self-Criticism*. London: New Left Books, 1976.

American Institute of Certified Public Accountants. *Objectives of Financial Statements: Report of the Study Group on the Objectives of Financial Statements*. New York: American Institute of Certified Public Accountants, 1973.

American Institute of Certified Public Accountants. *Objectives of Financial Statements: Volume 2, Selected Papers*. Joe J. Cramer, Jr. and George H. Sorter (eds.). New York: American Institute of Certified Public Accountants, 1974.

Amin, Samir. *The Law of Value and Historical Materialism*. New York: Monthly Review Press, 1978.

Armstrong, P. "Changing Management Control Strategies: The Role of Competition Between Accountancy and Other

---

Note: Both the American and British conventions of recording references were utilized in order to provide the maximum amount of information available.

Organizational Professions." *Accounting, Organizations and Society*, 1985, pp. 129–148.

Armstrong, P. "The Rise of Accounting Controls in British Capitalist Enterprises." *Accounting, Organizations and Society*, 1987, pp. 415–436.

Arrington, C. E. and Francis, J. R. "Letting the Chat Out of the Bag: Deconstruction, Privilege, and Accounting Research." *Accounting, Organizations and Society*, 1989a, pp. 1–24.

_____. "Accounting and the Labor of Text Production: Some Thoughts on the Hermeneutics of Paul Ricoeur." Presented at the *Conference on Accounting and the Humanities—The Appeal of Other Voices*, University of Iowa, 1989b.

Arrow, K. J. *Essays in the Theory of Risk Bearing.* Chicago: Markham, 1971.

Ball, R. and Brown, P. "An Empirical Evaluation of Accounting Income Numbers." *Journal of Accounting Research,* Autumn 1968, pp. 1–38.

Baran, Paul A. and Sweezy, Paul M. *Monopoly Capital.* New York: Monthly Review Press, 1966.

Baritz, Loren. *The Servants of Power: The Use of Social Science in American Industry.* New York: Wiley, 1960.

Barone, Charles A. "Samir and the Theory of Imperialism: A Critical Analysis." *The Review of Radical Political Economics,* Spring 1982, pp. 10–23.

Barthes, R. *Mythologies.* London: Jonathan Cape, 1972.

Beaver, W. "The Behavior of Security Prices and Its Implications for Accounting Research (Methods)." In *Supplement to The Accounting Review,* 1972, pp. 407–437.

_____. "The Information Content of the Magnitude of Unexpected Earnings." Unpublished manuscript, presented at Stanford Research Seminar, 1974.

Beaver, W. and Demski, J. "The Nature of Financial Accounting Objectives." In *Studies on Financial Accounting Objectives: 1974,* supplement to the *Journal of Accounting Research,* 1974, pp. 170–187.

Bell, S. *And We Are Not Saved: The Elusive Quest for Racial Justice.* New York: Basic Books, 1987.

Benston, George J. "Published Corporate Accounting Data and Stock Prices." In *Empirical Research in Accounting: Selected Studies 1967*, supplement to the *Journal of Accounting Research*, 1967, pp. 1–54.

_____. "Required Disclosure and the Stock Market: An Evaluation of the Securities Exchange Act of 1934." *American Economic Review*, March 1973, pp. 132–155.

_____. "The Market for Public Accounting Services: Demand, Supply and Regulation." *The Accounting Journal*, vol. 2, 1979/80, pp. 2–46.

_____. "Accounting and Corporate Accountability." *Accounting, Organizations and Society*, vol. 7, no. 2, 1982a, pp. 87–105.

_____. "An Analysis of the Role of Accounting Standards for Enhancing Corporate Governance and Solid Responsibility." *Journal of Accounting and Public Policy*, vol. 1, 1982b, pp. 5–17.

Berelson. *Foundations of Behavioral Research*. New York: Holt, Rhinehart and Winston, 1954.

Berlin, Isaiah. "The Concept of Scientific History." In *Philosophical Analysis and History*. New York: Harper and Row, 1966.

Bernstein, Richard. *The Restructuring of Social and Political Theory*. Oxford: Basil Blackwell, 1976; London: Methuen and Co., Ltd., 1979.

_____.*Beyond Objectivism and Relativism: Science, Hermeneutics, and Praxis*. Philadelphia: University of Pennsylvania Press, 1983.

Bird, John. "Jacques Lacan—The French Freud." *Radical Philosophy*, vol. 30, Spring 1982, pp. 7–13.

Blackburn, Robin (ed.). *Ideology in Social Science: Readings in Critical Social Theory*. New York: Pantheon Books, 1972.

Blanke, B., Jurgens, U., and Kastendiek. "On the Current Marxist Discussion on the Analysis of Form and Function of the Bourgeois State." In *State and Capital: A Marxist Debate*, John Holloway and Sol Picciotto (eds.). Austin: University of Texas Press, 1978.

Blaug, Mark. *The Methodology of Economics*. Cambridge: Cambridge University Press, 1980.

Bluestone, Barry and Harrison, Bennett. *The Deindustrialization of America: Plant Closings, Community Abandonment, and the Dismantling of Basic Industry.* New York: Basic Books, 1982.

Blumler, J. and Gurevitch, M. "The Political Effects of Mass Communication." In *Culture, Society and Media*, M. Gurevitch, T. Bennett, J. Curren, and J. Woollacott (eds.). London: Methuen and Co., 1982.

Boland, Richard J., Jr. "Myth and Technology in the American Accounting Profession." *Journal of Management Studies*, vol. 19, no. 1, 1982, pp. 109–127.

Briloff, Abraham. J. *The Truth About Corporate Accounting.* New York: Harper and Row, 1981.

_____. "Accountancy and Society: A Covenant Desecrated." *Critical Perspectives on Accounting*, March 1990, pp. 5–30.

Burchell, S., Clubb, C., Hopwood, A. G., and Naphapiet, J. "The Roles of Accounting in Organizations and Society." *Accounting, Organizations and Society*, 1980, pp. 5–28.

Burrell, G. and Morgan, G. *Sociological Paradigms and Organizational Analysis: Elements of the Sociology of Corporate Life.* London: Heinemann, 1979.

Campen, James T. and MacEwan, Arthur. "Crisis, Contradictions, and Conservative Controversies in Contemporary U.S. Capitalism." *Review of Radical Political Economics*, vol. 14, no. 3, Fall 1982, pp. 1–22.

Canning, J. *The Economics of Accountancy.* New York: Ronald Press, 1929.

Chambers, Ian. "Roland Barthes: Structuralism/Semiotics." In *Working Papers in Cultural Studies*, vol. 6, 1974.

Chambers, Raymond. *Accounting, Education and Economic Behavior.* Englewood Cliffs, NJ: Prentice Hall, 1966.

Chatfield, Michael. *The English View of Accountant's Duties and Responsibilities.* New York: Arno Press, 1978.

Chen, Rosita S. "Social and Financial Stewardship." *The Accounting Review*, July 1975, pp. 535–543.

Chenoweth, Lawrence. *The American Dream of Success: The Search for the Self in the Twentieth Century.* North Scituate, MA: Duxbury Press, 1974.

Christenson, Charles. "The Methodology of Positive Accounting." *Accounting Review*, vol. 53, January 1983, pp. 1–22.

Chua, W. F. "Radical Developments in Accounting Thought." *The Accounting Review*, October 1986, pp. 601–632.

_____. "Interpretive Sociology and Management Accounting Research." *Accounting, Auditing and Accountability*, 1988, pp. 59–79.

Ciancanelli, P. "Exchange, Reproduction and Sex Subordination Among the Kikuyu of East Africa." *The Review of Radical Political Economics*, vol. 12, no. 2, Summer 1980.

Cohen, K. and Cyert, R. M. *Theory of the Firm: Resource Allocation in a Market Economy*, 2nd ed. Englewood Cliffs, NJ: Prentice Hall, 1975.

Cohen G. A. *Karl Marx's Theory of History: A Defense*. Oxford: Clarendon Press, 1978.

_____. "Freedom, Justice and Capitalism." *New Left Review*, no. 126, March/April 1981, pp. 3–17.

Collins, D. W. "SEC Product-Line Reporting and Market Efficiency." *Journal of Financial Economics*, June 1975, pp. 125–164.

Coontz, S. and Henderson, P. (eds.). *Women's Work, Men's Property: The Origins of Gender and Class*. London: Verso, 1986.

Cooper, David. "Towards a Political Economy of Accounting: A Comment." *Accounting, Organizations and Society*, vol. 5, no. 1, 1980a, pp. 147–160.

_____. "Shareholder Power and Corporate Behavior." Unpublished dissertation, University of Manchester, 1980b.

_____. "A Social and Organizational View of Management Accounting." In *Essays in British Accounting Research*, M. Bromwich and A.G. Hopwood (eds.). London: Pitman, 1981.

_____. "Tidiness, Muddle and Things: Commonalities and Divergencies in Two Approaches to Management Accounting Research." *Accounting, Organizations and Society*, 1983, pp. 269–286.

_____. "A Political Economy of the UK Accounting Profession." Working paper, University of East Anglia, 1984.

Cornforth, Maurice Campbell. *The Theory of Knowledge*. vol. 3. New York: International Publishers, 1955, Revised 1963, 1971, 1973.

_____. *Communism and Philosophy: Contemporary Dogmas and Revisions of Marxism*. London: Lawrence and Wishart, 1980.

Coward, R. *Patriarchal Precedents: Sexuality and Social Relations*. London: Routledge and Kegan Paul, 1983.

Coward, R. and Ellis, J. *Language and Materialism: Developments in Genealogy and The Theory of the Subject*. London: Routledge and Kegan Paul, 1977.

Crouch, Colin (ed.). *State and Economy in Contemporary Capitalism*. New York: St. Martin's Press, 1979.

Curren, J., Gurevitch, M., and Woollacott, J. "The Study of the Media: Theoretical Approaches." In *Culture, Society and Media*, M. Gurevitch, T. Bennett, J. Curren, and J. Woollacott (eds.). London: Methuen and Co., 1982.

Dahl, R. A. *Democracy in the United States*. Chicago: Rand McNally, 1972.

Dale, R., Esland, G., and MacDonald, M. (eds.). *Schooling and Capitalism, A Sociological Reader*. London: The Open University Press, 1976.

Davis, Mike, "Why the U.S. Working Class is Different." *New Left Review*, no. 123, September/October 1980, pp. 3–44.

_____. "The New Right's Road to Power." *New Left Review*, no. 128, July/August 1981, pp. 28–49.

DeAngelo, L. E. "Managerial Competition, Information Costs, and Corporate Governance: The Use of Accounting Performance Measures in Proxy Contests." In *Journal of Accounting and Economics*, January 1988, pp. 3–36.

Demski, J. "Choice Among Financial Reporting Alternatives." *The Accounting Review*, April 1974, pp. 221–323.

Derrida, Jacques. *Of Grammatology*. Translated by Gayatri Chakravorty. Baltimore: Spivak, 1976.

_____. *Writing and Difference*. Translated by Alan Bass. Chicago: University of Chicago Press, 1978.

Dobb, Maurice. *Political Economy and Capitalism: Some Essays in Economic Tradition*. London: Routledge and Kegan Paul, 1937.

Dopuch, Nicholas. "Empirical vs. Non-Empirical Contributions to Accounting Theory Development." University of Alabama: University of Alabama Doctoral Consortium, 1980.

Doyal, Len and Harris, Roger. "The Practical Foundations of Human Understanding." *New Left Review*, no. 139, May/June 1982, pp. 59–78.

DuBoff, Richard B. and Herman, Edward S. "Alfred Chandler's New Business History: A Review." *Politics and Society*, vol. 10, no. 1, 1980, pp. 87–110.

Dukes, R. "An Investigation of the Effects of Expensing Research and Development Costs on Security Prices." Unpublished manuscript, Cornell University, 1975.

Dyckman, T. R., Downes, D. H., and Magee, R. P. *Efficient Capital Markets and Accounting: A Critical Analysis*. Englewood Cliffs, NJ: Prentice Hall, 1975.

Eagleton, Terry. *Criticism and Ideology: A Study in Marxist Literary Theory*. London: New Left Books, 1976.

Eco, Umberto. "Social Life as a Sign." In *Structuralism: An Introduction*. D. Rovey (ed.). Oxford: Clarendon Press, 1973.

Edgely, Roy. "Introduction to Derrida." *Radical Philosophy*, Spring 1979, pp. 20–34.

Edwards, R. S. *Contested Terrain: The Transformation of the Workplace in the Twentieth Century*. London: Heinemann, 1979.

Edwards, R. S. and Bell, P. *The Theory of Measurement of Business Income*. Berkeley: University of California Press, 1961.

Ellis, John. "Ideology and Subjectivity." In *Culture, Media and Language*, S. Hall, D. Hobson, A. Lowe, and P. Willis (eds.). London: Hutchinson, 1980.

Fama, E., Fisher, L., Jensen, M., and Roll, R. "The Adjustment of Stock Prices to New Information." *International Economic Review*, February 1969, pp. 1–21.

Fama, E. and Laffer, A. "Information and Capital Markets." *Journal of Business*, July 1971, pp. 289–298.

Fama, E. F. and Miller, M. H. *Theory of Finance.* New York: Holt, Rhinehart and Winston, 1972.

Feyerabend, Paul. K. "How to Be a Good Empiricist—A Plea For Tolerance In Matters Epsitemological." In *The Philosophy of Science.* P. H. Nidditch (ed.). Oxford: Oxford University Press, 1968.

———. "Against Method: Outline of An Anarchistic Theory of Knowledge." In *Minnesota Studies in the Philosophy of Science,* vol. 4. Michael Radner and Stephen Winokur (eds.). Minneapolis: University of Minnesota Press, 1970.

Financial Accounting Standards Board. "Statement of Financial Accounting Concepts No. 1: Objectives of Financial Reporting by Business Enterprises." Stamford, Conn.: Financial Accounting Standards Board, November 1978.

Forrester, Jay W. "Innovation and the Economic Long Wave." Massachusetts Institute of Technology, Sloan School of Management, Paper No. D-2990-1, Systems Dynamics Group, 1978.

Foucault, M. *The Archaeology of Knowledge.* London: Tavistock, 1972.

French, M. *Beyond Power: On Women, Men and Morals.* London: Abacus, 1986.

Galambos, L. The Public Image of Big Business in *America, 1880–1940, A Quantitative Study in Social Change.* Baltimore: Johns Hopkins University Press, 1975.

Galbraith, J. K. *The Great Crash.* Boston: Houghton Mifflin, 1954.

Gallhofer, S. and Haslam, J. "The Aura of Accounting in the Context of a Crisis: Germany and the First World War." *Accounting, Organizations and Society,* vol. 16, no. 5/6, 1991, pp. 487–520.

Gamble, A. and Walton, P. *Capitalism in Crisis.* London: Macmillan, 1976.

Gambling, Trevor. *Societal Accounting.* London: George Allen and Unwin, 1974.

George, Vic and Wilding, Paul. *Ideology and Social Welfare.* London: Routledge and Kegan Paul, 1976.

Gerbner, G., Holsti, O. R., Krippendorff, K., Paisley, W., and Stone, P. (eds.). *The Analysis of Communication Content*. New York: Wiley, 1969.

Geuss, Raymond. *The Idea of a Critical Theory: Habermas and The Frankfurt School*. Cambridge: Cambridge University Press, 1981.

Ghicas, D. and Tinker, T. "Dishonored Contracts: Accounting and the Expropriation of Employee Pension Wealth." Working paper, City University of New York, Baruch College, 1990.

Giddens, Anthony. *Central Problems in Social Theory: Action, Structure and Contradiction in Social Analysis*. Berkeley: University of California Press, 1979.

Gilligan, C. *In a Different Voice: Psychological Theory and Women's Development*. Cambridge, MA: Harvard University Press, 1982.

Gonedes, N. "Information Production and Capital Market Equilibrium." *Journal of Finance*, June 1975, pp. 841–864.

Gonedes, N. and Dopuch, N. "Capital Market Equilibrium, Information Production, and Selecting Accounting Techniques: Theoretical Framework and Review of Empirical Work." In *Studies on Financial Accounting Objectives 1974*, Supplement to the *Journal of Accounting Research*, 1974, pp. 48–129.

Gould, Stephen J. "Taxonomy as Politics: The Harm of False Classification." *Dissent*, Winter, 1990.

Gouldner, Alvin W. *The Dialectic of Ideology and Technology*. New York: The Seabury Press, 1976; Oxford: Oxford University Press, 1982a.

_____. *The Two Marxisms: Contradictions and Anomalies in the Development of Theory*. New York: The Seabury Press (Continuum), 1980; Oxford: Oxford University Press, 1982b.

Graaf, De, J. V. *Theoretical Welfare Economics*. Cambridge: Cambridge University Press, 1975.

Gramsci, A. *Selection from the Prison Notebooks*. London: Lawrence and Wishart, 1971.

Gray, R., Owen, D., and Maunders, K. *Corporate Social Reporting: Accounting and Accountability*. Hemel Hempstead: Prentice Hall, 1987.

Habermas, Jurgen. *Technology and Science As Ideology*. Frankfort: Main, 1969.

_____. *Towards a Rational Society*. Translated by Jeremy J. Shapiro. Boston: Beacon Press, 1970.

_____. *Theory and Practice*. Translated by John Viertel. Boston: Beacon Press, 1973.

_____. *Legitimation Crisis*. Translated by Thomas McCarthy. Boston: Beacon Press, 1975.

_____. *Communication and the Evolution of Society*. Translated by Thomas McCarthy. Boston: Beacon Press, 1979.

_____. "Conservatism and Capitalist Crisis." In *New Left Review*, no. 115, May/June 1979, pp. 72–86.

Hall, S. "Popular Democratic versus Authoritarian Popularism." In *Marxism and Democracy*, A. Hunt (ed.). London: Lawrence and Wishart, 1980a.

_____. "Cultural Studies at the Centre: Some Problematics and Problems." In *Culture, Media and Language*, S. Hall, D. Hobson, A. Lowe, and P. Willis (eds.). London: Hutchinson, 1980b.

_____. "The Rediscovery of Ideology: Return of the Repressed in Media Studies." In *Culture, Society and Media*, M. Gurevitch, T. Bennett, J. Curren, and J. Woollacott (eds.). London: Methuen & Co., 1982.

_____. "The Great Moving Right Show." In *The Politics of Thatcherism*, S. Hall and M. Jacques (eds.). London: Lawrence and Wishart, 1983a.

_____. "The Little Caesars of Social Democracy." In *The Politics of Thatcherism*, S. Hall and M. Jacques (eds.). London: Lawrence and Wishart, 1983b.

_____. "Thatcherism: Rolling Back the Welfare State." *Thesis Eleven*, no. 7 1983c, pp. 309–22.

Hall, S., Critcher, C., Jefferson, T., Clarke, J., and Roberts, B. *Policing the Crisis: Mugging, the State, and Law and Order*. London: Macmillan, 1978.

Haraway, Donna. *Primate Visions: Gender, Race and Nature in the World of Modern Science*. New York: Routledge, 1989.

Harcourt, G. C. "Some Cambridge Controversies in the Theory of Capital." *Journal of Economic Literature*, 1969, pp. 369–405.

Hatfield, H. R. *Modern Accounting: Its Principles and Some of its Problems.* New York: D. Appleton and Co., 1909.

Heck, M. C. "The Ideological Dimensions of Media Messages." In *Culture, Media and Language*, S. Hall, D. Hobson, A. Lowe, and P. Willis (eds.). London: Hutchinson, 1980.

Heilbroner, Robert L. *The Making of Economic Society.* Englewood Cliffs, NJ: Prentice Hall, 1980.

Held, D. *Introduction to Critical Theory: Horkheimer to Habermas.* London: Hutchinson, 1980.

Heydebrand, Wolf. "Critical Issues in Organizations" In Clegg, S. and Dunkerley, D. book review, *Administrative Science Quarterly* vol. 23, no. 4, 1978, pp. 640–645.

Heydebrand, Wolf and Burris, Beverly. "The Limits of Praxis in Critical Theory." Paper presented at the Annual Meeting of the American Sociological Association, New York, 1980.

Hill, Stephen. *Competition and Control At Work: The New Industrial Sociology.* London: 1981; Cambridge, Mass: The MIT Press, 1981.

Hindess, Barry and Hirst, Paul. *Mode of Production and Social Formation: An Anti-Critique of Pre-Capitalist Modes of Production.* New York: Macmillan, 1977.

Hines, R. "Popper's Methodology of Falsification and Accounting Research." *The Accounting Review*, October 1988a, pp. 657–62.

_____. "Financial Accounting: In Communicating Reality, We Construct Reality." *Accounting, Organizations and Society*, vol. 13, no. 3, 1988b, pp. 251–262.

_____. "The Sociopolitical Paradigm in Financial Accounting Research." *Accounting, Auditing and Accountability*, vol. 2, no. 2, 1989.

Hirsch, J. "The State Apparatus and Social Reproduction: Elements of a Theory of the Bourgeois State." In *State and Capital: A Marxist Debate*, John Holloway and Sol Picciotto (eds.). Austin: University of Texas Press, 1978.

Hirsch, M. *The Mother/Daughter Plot: Narrative, Psychoanalysis, Feminism*. Bloomington: Indiana University Press, 1989.

Hirshleifer, J. "The Private and Social Value of Information and the Reward for Incentive Activity." *American Economic Review*, September 1971, pp. 561–574.

Hirst, P. Q. "Althusser's Theory of Ideology." *Economy and Society*, vol. 5, 1976.

Holloway, John and Picciotto, Sol. *State and Capital: A Marxist Debate*. Austin: University of Texas Press, 1978.

Hoogvelt, A. and Tinker, A.M. "The Role of the Colonial and Post-Colonial State in Imperialism." *The Journal of African Studies*, vol. 16, no. 1, 1978, pp. 1–13.

Hopper, T., Storey, J., and Willmott, H. "Accounting for Accounting: Towards the Development of a Dialectical View." *Accounting, Organizations and Society*, vol. 12, no. 5, 1987, pp. 437–465.

Hopper, T., Cooper, D. J., Capps, T., Lowe, E. A., and Mouristsen, J. "Financial Controls in the Labour Process." In *Managing the Labour Process*, D. Knights and H. Willmott (eds.). Hampshire: Grower, 1986.

Hopwood, Anthony G. "The Archaeology of Accounting Systems." Paper presented at the Conference on the Roles of Accounting in Organizations and Society, University of Wisconsin, July 1984.

_____. "The Tale of a Committee that Never Reported: Disagreements on Intertwining Accounting with the Social." *Accounting, Organizations and Society*, 1985, pp. 361–377.

Horkheimer, M. and Adorno, T. W. *The Dialectic of Enlightenment*. New York: Herder and Herder, 1972. Original Edition, 1944.

Hoskin, K. W. and Macve, R. H. "Accounting and the Examination: A Genealogy of Disciplinary Power." *Accounting, Organizations and Society* vol. 11, no. 2, 1986, pp. 105–136.

Hunt, E. K. *Property and Prophets: The Evolution of Economic Institutions and Ideologies*. New York: Harper and Row, 1980.

Hurst, James Willard. *The Legitimacy of the Business Corporation in the Law of the United States, 1780–1970*. Charlottesville: The University Press of Virginia, 1970.

Jaggar, A. *Feminist Politics and Human Nature*. Sussex: Harvester Press, 1983.

Jensen, Michael C. and Meckling, William H. "Theory of the Firm: Managerial Behavior, Agency Cost and Ownership Structure." *Journal of Financial Economics*, vol. 3, 1976, pp. 305–360.

_____. "Can the Corporation Survive?" Proceedings, *UCLA Conference on Regulation*, California, 1980.

Jessop, B. "The Transformation of the State in Postwar Britain." In *The State in Western Europe*, R. Scase (ed.). New York: St. Martin's Press, 1980.

_____. *The Capitalist State: Marxist Theories and Methods*. London: Martin Robertson, 1982.

Jessop, B., Bonnett, K., and Bromley, S. "Authoritarian Popularism, Two Nations and Thatcherism." *New Left Review*, no. 147, September/October 1984, pp. 32–60.

Johnson, P. "From Virginia Woolf to the Post Moderns: Developments in a Feminist Aesthetic." *Radical Philosophy*, vol. 45, 1987, pp. 23–31.

Joseph, G. and Lewis, J. *Common Differences: Conflicts in Black and White Feminist Perspectives*. Boston: South End Press, 1981.

Katouzian, Homa. *Ideology and Method in Economics*. New York: Macmillan, 1980.

Katz, B. and Katz, L. S. *Magazines for Libraries*. New York: R. R. Bowker, 1977, 1982.

Keidel, Robert W. "Theme Appreciation as a Construct for Organizational Change." *Management Science*, 1981, pp. 1261–1278.

Kerlinger, Fred. *Content Analysis: Foundations of Behavioral Research*. New York: Holt, Rinehart and Winston, 1973.

Kessler-Harris, A. *Women Have Always Worked: An Historical Overview*. New York: McGraw-Hill, 1981.

Key, V. O., Jr. *Public Opinion and American Democracy*. New York: Knopf, 1967.

Knights, D. "Insuring Subjectivity: Reflections on the Subject and its Production in and Through State, City, and Financial Practices." University of Manchester Institute of Science and Technology, 1985.

Knights, D. and Collinson, D. "Disciplining the Shop Floor: A Comparison of the Disciplinary Effects of Managerial Psychology and Financial Accounting." *Accounting, Organizations and Society*, vol. 12, no. 5, 1987, pp. 457–478.

Knights, D. and Willmott, H. "Power and Identity in Theory and Practice." *The Sociological Review*, 1985, pp. 22–46.

Kohler, Eric. "The Goal of Accounting Education." American Institute of Accountants, "Extensions of Auditing Procedures," 1940, pp. 84–88.

Kolko, Gabriel. *The Triumph of Caonservatism: A Reinterpretation of American History, 1900–1916*. London: Collier-MacMillan, Ltd., 1963.

Kuhn, Thomas S. *The Structure of Scientific Revolutions*, 2nd ed. Chicago: University of Chicago Press, 1970.

Lacan, J. *Ecrits, A Selection*. London: Tavistock Publications, 1977.

Laclau, E. *Politics and Ideology in Marxist Theory*. London: New Left Books, 1977.

Laughlin, Richard C. "The Design of Accounting Systems: A Methodological Approach Based on Critical Theory and Some Insights Into Its Application in an Empirical Study of the Church of England." Working paper, University of Sheffield, January 1985.

_____. "Accounting Systems in Organizational Contexts: A Case for Critical Theory." *Accounting, Organizations and Society*, vol. 12, no. 5, 1987, pp. 479–502.

Lehman, C. "Accounting Ethics: Surviving Survival of the Fittest." *Advances in Public Interest Accounting*, vol. 2, 1988, pp. 71–82.

_____. "The Importance of Being Ernest: Gender Conflict in Accounting." *Advances in Public Interest Accounting*, vol. 3, 1990.

_____. "Herstory in Accounting: The First Eighty Years." *Accounting, Organizations and Society*, vol. 17, no. 2/3, 1992, pp. 261–285.

Lehman, C. and Tinker, T. "The 'Real' Cultural Significance of Accounts." *Accounting, Organizations and Society*, vol. 12, no. 5, 1987, pp. 503–522.

Lerner, G. *The Creation of Patriarchy*. New York: Oxford University Press, 1986.

Levi-Strauss, C. *The Scope of Anthropology*. London: Jonathan Cape, 1977.

Levy, H. "Portfolio Performance and the Investment Horizon." *Management Science*, August 1972, pp. 645–653.

Lindblom, Charles E. *Politics and Markets: The World's Political Economic Systems*. New York: Basic Books, 1977.

_____. "Another State of Mind." Presidential address, American Political Science Association, 1981. *American Political Science Review*, March 1982, pp. 9–21.

Littleton, A. C. and Zimmerman, V. K. *Accounting Theory, Continuity and Change*. Englewood Cliffs, NJ: Prentice Hall, 1962.

Lodge, George C. *The New American Ideology*. New York: Knopf, 1975.

Loft, A. "Toward a Critical Understanding of Accounting: The Case of Cost Accounting in the UK, 1914–1925." *Accounting, Organizations and Society*, 1986.

Lowe, E. A., Puxty, A.G. and Laughlin, R.C. "Simple Theories for Complex: Accounting Policy and the Market for Myopia." *Journal of Accounting and Public Policy*, Spring 1983, pp. 19–42.

Lowe E. A. and Tinker, A. M. "Sighting the Accounting Problematic: Towards an Intellectual Emancipation of Accounting." *Journal of Business Finance and Accounting*, vol. 4, no.3, 1975, pp. 263–276.

Lowi, Theodore, J. *The End of Liberalism: The Second Republic of the U.S.*, 2nd ed. New York: W.W. Norton, 1979.

Mandel, Ernest. *Late Capitalism*. London: New Left Books, 1975.

Marcuse, Herbert. *One-Dimensional Man: Studies in the Ideology of Advanced Industrial Society*. Boston: Beacon Press, 1964; Beacon Paperback, 1966.

Marshall, Alfred *Principles of Economics*, 8th ed. London: Macmillan and Co., 1920.

Marshall, J. "Private Incentives and Public Information." *American Economic Review,* June 1974, pp. 373–390.

Marx, Karl. *Capital: Volume One*. New York: Random House, 1977 (Original 1867).

Masterman, M. "The Nature of a Paradigm." In *Criticism and the Growth of Knowledge*. Imre Lakatos and Alan Musgrave (eds.). Cambridge: Cambridge University Press, 1970.

Mautz, R. K. "Where Do We Go From Here?." *The Accounting Review*, July 1974, pp. 353–360.

May, George O. *Financial Accounting: A Distillation of Experience*. Texas: Scholars Book Co., 1936.

McCraw, Thomas K. "Regulation in America: A Review Article." In *Business History Review*, Summer 1975, pp. 159–183.

McCarthy, Thomas. *The Critical Theory of Jurgen Habermas*. Cambridge, MA: MIT Press, 1978; Paperback edition, 1981.

McClelland, David C. *The Achieving Society*. New York: D. Van Nostrand Co, 1961.

Merino, Barbara D. and Neimark, Marilyn D. "Disclosure Regulation and Public Policy: A Sociohistorical Reappraisal." *Journal of Accounting and Public Policy*, vol. 1, 1982, pp. 33–57.

Miliband, Ralph. *The State in Capitalist Society: An Analysis of the Western System of Power*. New York: Basic Books, 1969.

Miller, P. and O'Leary, T. "Accounting and the Construction of the Governable Person." *Accounting, Organizations and Society*, vol. 12, no. 3, 1987, pp. 235–265.

Mitchell, Wesley C. *Business Cycles: The Problem and Its Setting*. New York: National Bureau of Economic Research, 1965.

Moore, David C. "Accounting on Trial: The Critical Legal Studies Movement and its Lessons for Radical Accounting." *Accounting, Organizations and Society,* vol. 16, no. 8, 1991, pp. 763–791.

Mosley, Hugh. "Capital and the State: West German Neo-Orthodox State Theory." *The Review of Radical Political Economics*, Spring 1982, pp. 24–33.

Neimark, Marilyn D. "The Social Construction of Annual Reports: A Radical Approach to Corporate Control." Unpublished doctoral dissertation, New York University, 1983.

_____. "The King is Dead. Long Live the King!" *Critical Perspectives on Accounting*, March 1990, pp. 103–114.

Oakes, Leslie and Hammond, Theresa. "Feminist Perpsectives on Science and Their Implications for Accounting Technologies." Working paper, University of Alberta, Edmonton, 1991.

O'Connor, James. *The Fiscal Crisis of the State*. New York: St. Martin's Press, 1975.

Offe, C., *Contradictions of the Welfare State*. John Keane (ed.). Cambridge, MA: MIT Press, 1984.

Okcabol, F. "Dismantling Financial Disclosure Regulations: An Empirical Test of the Stigler-Benston Hypothesis." Working paper, Hofstra University, 1989.

Okcabol, F., and Tinker, T. "The Market for Positive Theory: Deconstructing the Theory for Excuses." *Advances in Public Interest Accounting*, vol. 3, 1990.

Ollman, Bertell. *Alienation: Marx's Conception of Man in Capitalist Society*, 2nd ed. Cambridge: Cambridge University Press, 1976.

Panitch, Leo. "Trade Unions and the State." *New Left Review*, no. 125, January/February 1981, pp. 21–44.

Parker, L. D. "Polemical Themes in Social Accounting: A Scenario for Standard Setting." *Advances in Public Interest Accounting*, 1986, pp. 67–93.

Patell, J. "Corporate Forecasts of Earnings Per Share and Stock Price Behavior: Empirical Tests." Unpublished, 1976.

Pateman, C. *The Sexual Contract*. Stanford: Stanford University Press, 1988.

Paton, W. *Accounting Theory*. New York: Ronald Press, 1922.

Payer, Cheryl. *Lent and Lost: Foreign Credit and Third World Development*. London: Zed Books, 1991.

Peltzman, Sam. "Toward a More General Theory of Regulation." *Journal of Law and Economics*, 1976, pp. 211–240.

Pirsig, Robert M. *Zen and the Art of Motorcycle Maintenance: An Inquiry into Values*. New York: William Morrow, 1974.

Piven, F. F. and Coward, R. A. *Regulating the Poor: The Functions of Public Welfare*. New York: Pantheon Books, 1971.

Piven, F. F. and Coward, R. A. *The New Class War*. New York: Pantheon Books, 1982.

Plamenatz, John. *Ideology*. London: Pall Mall Press, 1970.

Pollard, Sidney. *The Genesis of Modern Management: A Study of The Industrial Revolution in Great Britain*. Middlesex, England: Penguin Books, 1968.

Popper, Karl R. *The Poverty of Historicism*. London: Routledge and Kegan Paul, 1957.

_____. *The Logic of Scientific Discovery*. London: Hutchinson and Co., 1959.

_____. *Conjectures and Refutations: The Growth of Scientific Knowledge*. New York: Harper Torchbooks, 1965.

_____. "The Logic of the Social Sciences." In *Positivist Dispute in German Sociology*, T. W. Adorno, et al. (eds.). London: Heinemann, 1976.

Posner, Richard A. "Theories of Economic Regulation." *The Bell Journal of Economics and Management Science*, Autumn 1974, pp. 335–358.

Post, Charles. "The American Road to Capitalism." *New Left Review*, no. 133, May/June 1982, pp. 30–52.

Potter, David M. "Explicit Data and Implicit Assumptions in Historical Study." In *Essays of David M. Potter*, Don E. Fehrenbacher (ed.). New York: Oxford University Press, 1973.

Poulantzas, Nicos. *Classes in Contemporary Capitalism*. Translated by David Fernback. London: New Left Books, 1975; London: Verso, 1978.

_____. *State, Power, Socialism*. London: New Left Books, 1978.

Poulantzas, Nicos and Miliband, Ralph. "The Problems of the Capitalist State." In *Ideology in Social Science: Readings in Critical Social Theory*, Robin Blackburn (ed.). New York: Pantheon Books, 1972.

Previts, Gary J. and Merino, Barbara D. *A History of Accounting in America: An Historical Interpretation of the Cultural Significance of Accounting*. New York: Wiley, 1979.

Puxty, Anthony G. "Locating the Accounting Profession in the Class Structure: Evidence from the Growth of the User

Criterion for Financial Statements." Sheffield: University of Sheffield, November 1984.

Ravetz, J. "Ideological Commitments in the Philosophy of Science." *Radical Philosophy*, 37, Summer 1984, pp. 5–11.

Robinson, Joan. "The Production Function and the Theory of Capital." *Review of Economic Studies*, 21, 1953–54, pp. 81–106.

Ronen, J. "The Effect of Insider Trading Rules on Information and Disclosure by Corporations." *The Accounting Review*, April 1977, pp. 438–449.

———. "The Dual Role of Accounting: A Financial Economic Perspective." In *Handbook of Financial Economics,* James L. Bicksler (ed.). North Holland, 1979, pp. 415–454.

Ronen, J. and Sorter, G. "A Note on Accounting Alternatives and Social Choice." In *Relevant Financial Statements.* New York: Arno Press, 1978.

Rose, Hilary and Rose, Steven. *Science and Society.* New York: Penguin Books, 1969; Reprinted, 1977.

Rowthorn, Bob. "Late Capitalism." *New Left Review*, no. 98, July/August 1976, pp. 59–83.

Rubenstein, M. "Securities Market Efficiency in an Arrow-Debreu Economy." *American Economic Review*, December 1975, pp. 812–824.

Rude, George. *Ideology and Popular Protest.* New York: Pantheon Books, 1980.

Ryan, M. *Marxism and Deconstruction: A Critical Articulation.* Baltimore: Johns Hopkins University Press, 1982.

Samuelson, Paul A. "A Summing Up." In "Paradoxes in Capital Theory: A Symposium." *Quarterly Journal of Economics*, vol. 80, November 1966.

Samuelson, Paul A. *Economics,* 8th ed. New York: McGraw Hill, 1984.

Sassoon, Anne Showstack. "Hegemony and Political Intervention." In *Politics, Ideology and the State*, Sally Hibblin (ed.). London: Lawrence and Wishart, 1978.

Saussure, F. de. *A Course in General Linguistics.* London: P. Owen, 1960.

Scott, DR. *The Cultural Significance of Accounts.* Lawrence, KS: Scholars Book Club, 1931.

Seliger, Martin. *The Marxist Conception of Ideology: A Critical Essay.* Cambridge: Cambridge University Press, 1979.

Shaikh, A. "The Current World Economic Crises: Causes and Implications." Working paper, New York University, 1983.

Shaw, Martin. *Marxism and Social Science: The Roots of Social Knowledge.* London: Pluto Press, 1975.

Shrivastava, Paul. "A Critique of the Image and Ideals of Strategic Management." Working paper, New York University, 1983.

Spacek, L. "A Suggested Solution to the Principles Dilemma." *The Accounting Review,* 1964, pp. 275–284.

Sraffa. P. *The Production of Commodities by Means of Commodities: Prelude to a Critique of Economic Theory.* Cambridge: Cambridge University Press, 1960.

Sterling, Robert (ed.). *Institutional Issues in Public Accounting.* Lawrence, KS: Scholars Book Co., 1974.

Stiehm, J. (ed.). *Women's Views of the Political World of Men.* New York: Transnational Publishers, 1984.

Stigler, G. J. "The Theory of Economic Regulation." *The Bell Journal of Economics and Management Science,* Spring 1971, pp. 3–21.

Stiglitz, J. "Some Aspects of the Pure Theory of Corporate Finance: Bankruptcies and Take-Overs." *The Bell Journal of Economics and Management Science,* Autumn 1972, pp. 458–481.

Sunder, Shyam. "Why is the FASB Making Too Many Accounting Rules?" *Managers Journal: Wall Street Journal,* April 27, 1981, p. 30.

Sutton, F.X., Harris, S.E., Kaysen,C., and Tobin,J. *The American Business Creed.* Cambridge, MA: Harvard University Press, 1956.

Therborn, Goran. *The Ideology of Power and the Power of Ideology.* London: Verso, 1980.

Thompson, John B. "Rationality and Social Rationalization: An Assessment of Habermas's Theory of Communicative Action." *Sociology,* vol. 17 no. 2, May 1983, pp. 278–294.

Tigar, Michael E. and Levy, Madeleine R. *Law and the Rise of Capitalism*. New York: Monthly Review Press, 1977.

Tinker, Anthony. "Theories of the State and the State of Accounting: Economic Reductionism and Political Voluntarism in Accounting Regulation Theory." *Journal of Accounting and Public Policy*, vol. 3, 1984, pp. 55–74.

Tinker, A. M. "Towards a Political Economy of Accounting: An Empirical Illustration of the Cambridge Controversies." *Accounting, Organizations and Society*, vol. 5, no. 1, 1980, pp.147–160.

Tinker, A.M., Merino, B., and Neimark, M.D. "The Normative Origins of Positive Theories: Ideology and Accounting Thought." *Accounting, Organizations and Society*, vol.7, no. 2, 1982, pp. 167–200.

Tinker, Tony (ed.). *Social Accounting: Private Enterprise versus the Public Interest*. New York: Markus Weiner Publishing, 1984.

_____. *Paper Prophets: A Social Critique of Accounting*. New York: Praeger Publishers, 1985.

_____. "The Accountant as Partisan." *Accounting, Organizations and Society*, vol. 16, no. 3, 1991, pp. 297–310.

Tinker, T., Lehman, C., and Neimark, M. "Bookkeeping for Capitalism: The Mystery of Accounting for Unequal Exchange." In *The Political Economy of Information*, V. Mosco and J. Wasko (eds). Wisconsin: University of Wisconsin Press, 1988.

_____. "Falling Down the Hole in the Middle-of-the-Road: Political Quietism in Corporate Social Reporting." *Accounting, Auditing and Accountability*, vol. 4, no. 2, 1991, pp. 28–54.

Watts, R. and Zimmerman, J. "Toward a Positive Theory of the Determination of Accounting Standards." *The Accounting Review*, vol. 53, no. 1, January 1978, pp. 112–134.

_____. "The Demand for and Supply of Accounting Theories: The Market for Excuses." *The Accounting Review*, vol. 54, no. 2, April 1979, pp.273–305.

_____. "Positive Accounting Theory: A Ten Year Perpsective." *The Accounting Review*, January 1990, pp. 131–156.

Weedon, C., Tolson, A., and Mort, F. "Theories of Language and Subjectivity." In *Culture, Media and Language*, S. Hall, D. Hobson, A. Lowe, and P. Willis (eds.). London: Hutchinson, 1980.

Weinstein, James. *The Corporate Ideal in the Liberal State, 1900–1918*. Boston: Beacon Press, 1968.

Whitley, Richard (ed.). *Social Process of Scientific Development*. London and Boston: Routledge and Kegan Paul, 1974.

Williams, Paul F. "A Descriptive Analysis of Authorship in *The Accounting Review*." *The Accounting Review*, vol. 60, no. 2, April 1985, pp. 300–313.

Willis, P. "Notes on Method." In *Culture, Media and Language*, S. Hall, D. Hobson, A. Lowe, and P. Willis (eds.). London: Hutchinson, 1980.

Winch, Peter. *The Idea of a Social Science and its Relation to Philosophy*. Atlantic Highlands, NJ: Humanities Press, 1958.

Wolfe, Alan. "Sociology, Liberalism and the Radical Right." *New Left Review*, no. 128, July/August 1981, pp. 3–28.

Woollacott, J. "Messages and Meaning." In *Culture, Society and Media*, M. Gurevitch, T. Bennett, J. Curren, and J. Woollacott (eds.). London: Methuen and Co., 1982.

Wright, Erik Olin. *Class, Crisis and the State*. London: New Left Books, 1978.

_____. "Alternative Perspectives in the Marxist Theory of Accumulation and Crisis." *The Insurgent Sociologist*, vol. 6, no. 1, Fall 1975, pp 5–39.

_____. "Class Boundaries in Advanced Capitalist Societies." *New Left Review*, no. 98, July/August 1976, pp. 3–42.

Zeff, S. A. "The Rise of Economic Consequence." *Journal of Accountancy*, December 1978, pp. 56–63.

_____. "Impact of Changes in the Profession: On the Debate Over Accounting Principles." Annual Meeting of the American Accounting Association, Reno, 1985.

Zukav, Gary. *The Dancing Wu Li Masters: An Overview of the New Physics*. New York: William Morrow and Co., 1979.